From Oz to Om

To: Bruce

There's no place like home!

Trevor Banks

From Oz To Om

The Spiritual Journey Home

Tracy Flynn Bowe

ISBNs: 978-0-9987069-0-0 (paperback); 978-0-9987069-1-7 (ePub); 978-0-9987069-2-4 (Kindle)

Library of Congress Catalog Number: 2017903746
Tracy Flynn Bowe, Sauk Rapids, Minnesota

Printed in the United States of America
First Printing: 2017
21 20 19 18 17   5 4 3 2 1

Cover and interior design by Ryan Scheife, Mayfly Design
Cover artwork: background sky © javarman/shutterstock; yellow brick wall texture © RAYphotographer/shutterstock; red glitter texture © mmkarabella/shutterstock

To order, visit www.tracybowe.com

To my mother Dorothy, who is my wise, compassionate and ever-present Glinda; To my sisters Kate and Meg who have been my faithful Lion and Tin Man; To my husband Jack who has been my steadfast Scarecrow, and to our children, Cady, Cully, Chris and Anne, who have helped me to grow through all the joys and the struggles of the path; To Carol, Chuck, Michelle and Sharon, who have played the part of Wizard when I needed one; And to my father Joe, and my brothers Mike and Chris, and all the teachers and friends with whom I have walked along my yellow brick road; Thank you all for your love, your light and your blessings, and for helping me to remember my Home in the Om.

Contents

Foreword

The journey to find one's Om begins with the simple question "Who Am I?" The moment we ask this question it's as if unknown doorways of the mind open. We experience a heightened sense of awareness, not only of ourselves and our lives, but of our experiences and the people who help create and add to those experiences. It's this awareness that sets off an avalanche of changes, shifts in perception and the expansion of our spiritual consciousness. It's this awareness that makes it possible for us to catch a glimpse of our soul and our true home within us—the Om.

As a result of our conditioning, we've been led to believe this journey we call life must be hard work and that we must experience struggle and strife to somehow find our way. We are taught that we must slay our fears rather than just seeing them from a renewed perspective. We are told that we must think, say and act like others so it's not obvious that we march to a different drummer. It's as if we've become afraid of being different, being unique and just plain being ourselves. However, the Om in us knows that all of this is merely illusion, cleverly designed to keep us safe and to keep our lives predictable. So the Om in us encourages us through its metaphors to walk the Yellow Brick road and find the parts of ourselves that have become lost along the way. Our Om inspires us to persevere and gently nudges us to find our inner truth so we may become whole and live healthy lives.

The connection between who we think we are and who we really are represents a cohesive integration between the soul and the mind. Yet the mind forgets this connection and instead sees itself separate from the soul, controlling who we are and limiting what we think we're capable of becoming. The Om in us encourages "transcending what the mind sees as opposites" so we're able to resolve the inner conflicts that hold us hostage to our past and our old ways of thinking. In this way we're able to transcend the perception that we're human beings having a spiritual experience and begin living our lives as spiritual beings having a human experience. This shift in perception alone transforms everyday consciousness into spiritual consciousness. Questions answer themselves, and our purpose on this earth becomes not only self-evident, it serves as a guiding light illuminating the way home, should we find ourselves feeling lost or alone in times of darkness.

In this book, *From Oz to Om*, Tracy Bowe masterfully uses the story and the metaphors found in *The Wizard of Oz* to help us see how fears and mental limitations hold us back. She helps us find our own heart as the Tin Man finds his heart, making it possible for us to be more open to loving ourselves and loving others. This book helps us find the courage to change and face our fears like the Cowardly Lion, who finds his courage. And it helps us find our Om brain and our spiritual consciousness, like the Scare Crow, who finds he already has a brain.

We all have wicked witches (fears) and we all have flying monkeys (limiting thoughts) that, if allowed, can and will stop us on our journey to the Emerald City (our higher selves). Yet like Dorothy, we're constantly being reminded by our soul that within each of us lies the ability we need in order to go home—if we just click the heels of our Ruby Slippers three times. Why three times? Because there are three parts of who we are: a mind, a body and a soul, and when they all work cooperatively, we can truly live up to our highest potential in our everyday lives.

This book is unique in that it includes exercises, tools and techniques that are designed to make the journey to Om more productive and joyful and less daunting and stressful. This wonderful book helps us remember who we really are. It provides the understanding needed so we can receive the blessings in our fears and can recognize the inner strength we carry inside to overcome those fears. This book teaches us how spiritual consciousness can guide us and help us navigate the obstacles that will appear as we move forward in our own personal journey to self. And, as with Dorothy, *From OZ to OM* reminds us that there's no place like home.

Carol Ritberger, Ph.D.
Author of *What Color Is Your Personality* and *Healing Happens With Your Help*

Introduction

*E*very now and then, a story touches us deeply and becomes a part of how we know ourselves in the world. *The Wizard of Oz* is such a story. Speaking to us across generations and across cultures, the characters from Oz came alive for a generation in one of the most beloved movies ever made. Today, over seventy-five years after the film's initial release, families still gather to watch Dorothy make her archetypal journey down the yellow brick road to meet the Wizard, to confront her fears, to defeat the Wicked Witch and ultimately to find her way home, awake to the essential wisdom and power resting within her heart.

The *Wizard of Oz* is a story of our times. It is big enough to hold the mystery of the universe, yet it is walked by a little girl from Kansas, one foot in front of the other, down the yellow brick road. As Dorothy's story draws to an end, it becomes evident that the *Wizard of Oz* is not only a story about an ordinary girl from Kansas on an extraordinary adventure but a story about the journey each of us takes when we begin to seek for deeper meaning in our lives.

The *Wizard of Oz* provides us a map of the universal spiritual journey as we walk with Dorothy to Oz and beyond. The spiritual journey can also be called *the Hero's Journey,* and Joseph Campbell, the great western mythologist, left us his own map of this universal journey. A third map of this journey can be found in the spiritual teachings of the eastern chakra system. The seven chakras represent our energy body, and we can follow the unfolding of the spiritual self through these chakra centers as well.

Blending the archetypal imagery of Oz with western mythology and the eastern spiritual teachings of the chakras, our attention to Dorothy's mystical experience in Oz takes us along on the hero's journey that we are all called to walk. The Oz story provides us with the metaphors and markers along the spiral journey of transformation as we walk the yellow brick road along with Dorothy. At the end of this journey, like Dorothy, we arrive home with the knowing that God resides within and that our home and our power rest within the essence of that powerful presence—we find our home in the *OM*.

This book is meant to provide both a descriptive and an experiential map of the hero's journey. You may wish to rewatch *The Wizard of Oz* before reading this book so that the storyline, characters, images and symbols are fresh in your imagination. Each chapter represents a stage in the hero's journey and begins with an anchoring meditation as context for the chapter. What follows each meditation is a description of each stage of the journey using the imagery of the Oz story, the anchors of Campbell's hero's journey and the wisdom of the seven-chakra system. The descriptions will call the reader to reflect on the symbols and metaphors from the movie version of Dorothy's epic journey and to see the spiritual teaching embedded in her extraordinary adventure to Oz. At the end of each chapter are *Stepping Stones*, questions for meditation and journaling that will invite you to focus on the mystery of your own adventures as you walk your own yellow brick road. You might also journal about the symbols and imagery of the story to allow it to unfold more deeply in your own experience.

It is my deep wish that through this process you will find yourself moving closer to your spiritual "home" and will catch glimpses of the beauty and grace of your being. This is a journey I have walked myself and continue to walk each day. You will find my teachers and guides throughout the pages of this book. My teachers have been authors and philosophers, mystics both ancient and modern, theologians, poets, priests, professors and psychologists. I have learned lessons with my husband, my children, my siblings and my parents. My path has been blessed by mentors and cheerleaders, naysayers and nemeses. I have had experiences of great joy and bliss, and moments of deep disappointment and trauma. But this is precisely the hero's journey. An ordinary life that moves through trials and tests to the unfolding of our spiritual center. I marvel at how every experience, the pleasant and the painful, the exhilarating and the fearful, the joys and the sorrows, were all used for my own awakening and timed to perfection—no experience was left behind, no turn in life was mistaken, no person along my path insignificant. The experiences I have had along my yellow brick road have allowed me to re-member the parts of myself that had been disconnected through the confusing, disappointing, fearful and traumatic experiences of life, and to remember the deeper unity that connects me in each moment and in each experience to my soul and to *All That Is*. I offer my profound gratitude to all who have walked with me on my journey—whether they have walked with me literally or have illuminated my path through their writings and teachings. It is my sincere hope and intention that this book will inspire others as they make their spiritual journey home.

The Hero's Journey

"The Privilege of a Lifetime Is Being Who You Are."

~ Joseph Campbell

*P*oet Mary Oliver asks us, "Tell me, what is it you plan to do with your one wild and precious life?" This is the central question of our existence, and yet it is one that many of us are afraid to ask, much less answer. Many of us are afraid to ask this question because like Dorothy in *The Wizard of Oz* we have been taught to play small. We have been encouraged to give up our dreams for our lives in favor of safer, more practical plans. For some, the fear comes from parents or loved ones who wanted to keep us safe and to spare us the disappointments and struggles of life. For some the fear comes from having dreams for ourselves that seem too big to be real. For others the fear comes from realizing that we've forgotten how to dream about life altogether. But the story of Dorothy reminds us that we are called to dream. We are each called to participate fully in the magic of our own life stories. We are called to connect our dreams and visions from "somewhere over the rainbow" to the lives we live each day.

But how do we come to understand the magic of our own life stories, the pure mystery of our own existence, or our divine nature in the midst of the cosmos? How do we find the courage and the will to live our lives with meaning and purpose, seeking and finding our heart's deepest desires? How do we say *no* to a culture that encourages us to live lives of quiet desperation, settling for boredom, consumerism, workaholism, addiction, disconnection and discontent, when we are meant to be on a wild and joyful adventure of our own making? These are the questions that we all grapple with as human beings, and yet the answers most often elude us as we become hypnotized by the trance of daily life and by the dictates of a culture that is immersed in stories of danger, fear, safety and survival.

Joseph Campbell, the preeminent teacher of world myths and metaphors, believed that myths served the critical function of providing us with stories that explore these central human questions. A myth is a teaching story that expresses in universal symbols the meaning of life, the struggles of human existence and the mystery of our connection to the universe. Myths and metaphors speak to our unconscious of the patterns of life and of the universe which our conscious minds don't always apprehend. Myths reawaken us to the epic nature of life as it unfolds around us, and they help us to see pieces of ourselves in the heroes and heroines of all times.

Campbell was most well known for his work on the hero's journey. Campbell taught that in every tradition and in every culture we find the myth of the hero's journey. The hero's journey is a myth about living our own adventure. It is the quest for the truth of our own nature as spiritual beings, for an understanding of our relationship to the divine and for our sacred purpose in the world. In western literature the hero's journey can be seen in the King Arthur legends and in the search for the Holy Grail. The search for the Holy Grail represents our search for our connection to soul. This search can be seen in the Jewish tradition in the story of Moses and the search for the "promised land." We can find it the East in the Bhagavad Gita's story of Arjuna's epic battle guided by Krishna. And in Christian literature we have the story of Jesus. All cultures and religious traditions have used mythic or sacred stories as a means to understand the human struggle with our own divinity and as a guide for understanding the human search for meaning.

In 20th century America we were given a new grail story in the myth of the Wizard of Oz. The story of Oz began with the book authored by L. Frank Baum in 1900, but this turn-of-the-century story soon became the motion picture marvel that has been seen by over a billion people around the world. We find in the story of Dorothy a feminine heroine who perhaps foreshadows the awakening of the feminine principle in this time. Dorothy is a hero for our times—in this heartwarming story we can find all the markers of the universal spiritual journey. Dorothy is an ordinary little girl from Kansas who goes on an extraordinary adventure and in the process discovers her own hero essence. Embedded in the magic and wonder of the Oz story is a modern version of the hero's journey, filled with symbols and metaphors that can help us all understand our search for meaning and deep belonging in our lives and in the universe.

One of the gifts of Joseph Campbell's work on the hero's journey is to provide us with a map of the universal quest we all make as human beings in the discovery of our own spiritual nature. Maps are useful in that they provide us with the landmarks along the journey so that we know where we are, what to be watching for and where we are going. The hero's journey, like all of life, unfolds in a predictable series of stages. The hero's journey is a spiritual quest that we will all take, one way or another, again and again, cycle after cycle. Familiarizing ourselves with the twists and turns of the journey can offer us some solace and repose as we wander and sometimes struggle along our own path, and it can offer us some opportunities to be more reflective and aware as we make our way. If we lay Campbell's map over the well-known tale of the Wizard of Oz, we can more clearly see the map of our own hero's journey illuminated through its metaphors and might more easily navigate along our own yellow brick road.

In the eastern traditions there is another map that helps us to chart our path to discovering our spiritual nature and living our truth in the world. It is the map of the chakra system. The eastern traditions teach us that we are souls temporarily residing in physical bodies that are literally pulsating from moment to moment with physical, emotional, mental and spiritual energy. This body of energy is rich with information regarding our inner life and supports us as we answer the call of our higher spiritual nature. The chakras are a map for understanding the connections between mind, body, emotions and spirit and are a tool for inner awareness and self-knowledge. In her *New York Times* best-seller book *Anatomy of the Spirit*, Carolyn Myss brilliantly introduces the map of the chakra system to the western world in a way that allows western readers to understand the chakras through our western sensibilities and religious traditions. This seven-chakra map can also be laid over the Wizard of Oz story, and the wisdom of the chakra energies can serve as additional markers along the hero's journey.

In western religious traditions our spiritual paths tend to lead us to a transcendent God. We are taught that the answers to life's struggles and challenges will be found through surrendering to the power and protection of an omnipotent God. In eastern traditions the spiritual journey peaks in the discovery of the unity between the spiritual nature of the individual and the Divine Field of Being that might be described as Om consciousness. Yet both eastern and western faith traditions teach us that we are more than physical beings—that we are always in connection with God, with the Divine that resides within. In order to discover this deep connection to All That Is, we must begin a journey to find our deepest self. Christian theologian Thomas Merton calls this self the *True Self*, Buddhists call it *Big Self*, Humanists call it *Self* or *Identity* and mystics call it the *Soul*. By whatever name, there is clearly a deep spiritual yearning at this time to connect with the God within, with our deep essence, with the Om, as a source of love, connection, guidance and belonging. Our search for Self is our search for our true home in the universe.

The Oz story provides a bridge from where most western religious traditions leave us in our spiritual search—in the throne room of the Great and Powerful Oz—to the inner Om consciousness that is at the heart of all wisdom and mystical traditions. As we walk with Dorothy through her epic journey home, we are led symbolically through the universal stages of the spiritual journey. We discover that we will find what we seek not outside of ourselves but rather within ourselves. This mythical story walks us along our own "yellow brick road" deep within ourselves to discover our true spiritual home.

In the blending of the maps provided by Joseph Campbell and the eastern chakras, the memorable characters of the Oz story provide rich images and charming metaphors for our imaginations to hang on to as we each walk our own yellow brick road from Oz to Om. Campbell urges us all to live from our own center. He calls this walk *following your bliss.* Based on the teachings of the universal myths, Campbell promises that if we just begin the walk toward our Self, the Universe will show up to meet us, and a path will open before us that is distinctly our own.

When the mystery of our own existence meets the Mystery of the Universe, truly extraordinary things come to pass. In the chapters that follow, the hero's journey, the chakras and the Oz story provide the signposts for journeying onto our sacred path in the world. It is my hope that the markers provided by this book will allow the reader to anchor her or his own life adventure on this path, to push through the challenges and struggles of life and to discover the wonder and joy of living from one's center, in connection with All That Is.

The Call

"Opportunities to Find Deeper Powers within Ourselves Come When
Life Seems Most Challenging."

~ JOSEPH CAMPBELL

In the first stage of the hero's journey there is a life event that calls
us into the mystery of our own story. Something happens, maybe
dramatic, maybe not, but in the wake of that event we know that
something has changed, or is about to change, whether we consciously invite it or not. The call is usually preceded by a time of
feeling uneasy, uncomfortable, discontented or downright discouraged with our current life story. We have a sense that we are not
living our life the way we intended or the way we had imagined
for ourselves. An inner longing is beginning to wake up inside of
us and is urging us toward something deeper, something bigger,
something grander for ourselves. The call may come forward subtly
in the form of depression, anxiety, a persistent feeling of dissatis-
faction, irritation or anger. Or the call may show up more dramatically through an intense conflict with a nemesis figure, the loss of
a job, the collapse of a marriage, a move to a new city, an illness,
or the loss of a loved one. Whatever the circumstances, the call
comes forward to wake us up from the unconsciousness of our daily
living, and invites us to participate in creating a bigger story for
ourselves. We can try to push this inner call away—we usually do
for a time—but most of us find the call into our own story persistent

and unyielding. The call will keep coming—the choice to follow or not, now or later, is ours.

---

*D*orothy begins her mythic journey on a small farm in Kansas, where nothing seems likely to change, despite her obvious discontent. The movie begins in black and white, with Dorothy dreaming of something beyond the shadows of her dreary Kansas farm life. The call begins when her faithful dog Toto is taken by an unwelcome visitor, the mean and frightening Elvira Gulch. According to Miss Gulch, Toto is disruptive, unruly and dangerously out of control. Under the gray Kansas sky of the opening scenes, Dorothy is called out of her doldrums and into the drama by her nemesis, Miss Gulch, who holds an order from the sheriff to seize her beloved Toto. In the midst of this crisis, Toto escapes from Miss Gulch and returns to Dorothy, who begins her journey following the lead of her dog, Toto, a theme that continues throughout the story. Toto metaphorically represents Dorothy's intuition, her internal guidance system that nudges and presses her along the path to find her true Self.

We learn from Dorothy's story that as we begin the hero's journey we do not always wake up from the hypnosis or unconsciousness of our rote day-to-day existence by ourselves. Most often it takes an experience in the outer world to get our attention. Perhaps we have been silently lamenting about the plight of our life in the months or years that precede the call, but have been unwilling to take those first steps on the path of our own hero's journey. Often the messenger that calls us to begin the journey is not perceived as a welcome visitor. We may be called into the drama as a seemingly unwilling participant in a personal or professional crisis. Perhaps it is a disruption in our marriage, our family life or our work life. Perhaps it is a conflict with another person that creates a great deal of discomfort or trauma in our life. Perhaps it is the loss of someone significant in our life. Perhaps it is an internal crisis of illness, depression or anxiety. But whether invited or not, the event occurs, and the drama begins.

The first step in the journey calls us to look more deeply at what is happening in our life. We may experience a sense of indignation or betrayal at having our lives upset, and yet it startles us out of our routine and forces us to take the first steps of our spiritual journey. We always have the choice to refuse the call and to stay embedded in the old and familiar patterns of our lives. The great myths teach us, however, that to refuse the call will lead to stagnation, to the loss of vital life energy and to the drying up of life. Hell, said Campbell, is the drying up of life. The myths also teach us that even if at first we refuse to begin our journey, inevitably the call persists, returning for us usually in more ferocious and negative forms.

The teaching of this stage of the hero's journey is that we will be called again and again back into the unfolding of our own story. The more we try to stay unconscious about our true purpose, and the more forcefully we resist moving out of our safe but often dreary and small lives, the more forcefully the call will come for us. Marion Woodman, a

Jungian analyst and psychological teacher, tells the story of her own analyst admonishing her that "the unconscious will take you where the unconscious will take you; you can either go squealing like a pig to the slaughter, or you can go with a little bit of dignity." Those who have traveled this path the hard way might suggest we answer the call with a little "bit of dignity," but we always have a choice.

The first steps we take on the hero's journey are usually not particularly conscious. We are following our intuition, that little voice inside that nudges, shoves or tugs us toward something new, just as Dorothy follows Toto. The mystics of all spiritual traditions teach us that the intuition is the guide to the soul. Intuition is the still, small voice that calls us into the mystery of our own story. The voice of our intuition does not shame us, frighten us or force us. It is a quiet awareness that draws us toward experiences that reflect our inner state of being. It tries to get our attention about the patterns in our lives that are not serving us. It tries to make conscious the parts of our lives that are out of alignment with our deeper truth or our greater purpose.

In the Oz myth Toto represents the intuition and will serve as Dorothy's faithful guide throughout the story. In truth it is Toto, the intuition, that initiates the journey to Oz. Elvira Gulch was right that Toto is disruptive, unruly and dangerous. Toto creates a disturbance in Dorothy's world, disrupting the calm, the quiet and the monotony of her Kansas farm life, drawing her unknowingly into a journey with the magical and the mystical story of her life.

Toto is the latin word for "whole," and Dorothy's faithful friend is calling her into wholeness.

This is the work of the soul, the invisible Self, to draw us into circumstances that provide us with the opportunity to experience, learn, grow and evolve in our understanding of ourselves and the universe. Our intuition, the voice of our higher Self, silently initiates our journey and creates the experiences that tease us toward a new way of seeing, experiencing, imagining or perhaps remembering ourselves. It's almost as if our intuition gives us a very quick glimpse behind the scenes of our intended life story. The glimpse is too fast to hold on to but long enough to remember that something important is happening here and long enough to tell us we need to wake up out of the unconsciousness of our ordinary existence and pay attention.

Stepping Stones

Awareness Affirmation: *My Intuition leads me toward new ways of being and living that support my growth and evolution. I trust this inner wisdom and say yes to the call of my soul.*

What events that have recently occurred in your life resonate with this part of the journey?

◎ Where have you noticed a feeling of restlessness or discontent in your life in the past months or years?

◎ What have you been secretly longing for in your heart?

◎ How has your intuition been speaking to you through these feelings and experiences?

◎ What tricks or distractions have you used to silence or mute this inner nudging?

◎ Who are the unwelcome visitors who may have entered your life lately and disrupted your routine?

◎ In what ways has the call become persistent?

◎ What parts of you feel indignant, betrayed or resistant to the call?

◎ What parts of you are waking up, changing or asking you to give them attention?

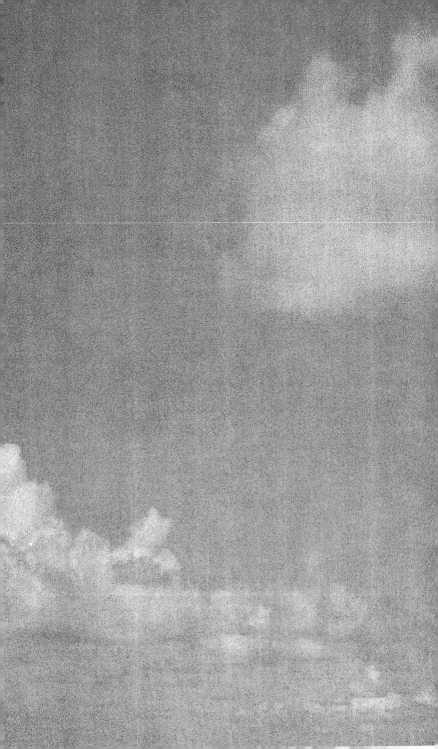

Dying to the Old

"We Must Be Willing to Get Rid of the Life We've Planned, So as to Have the Life That Is Waiting for Us."

~ JOSEPH CAMPBELL

In the next step on the hero's journey we awaken to the fact that a familiar life pattern has been outgrown. We find that the old concepts, ideals and emotional patterns that have organized our life no longer serve us. It begins to feel as though the life we have constructed for ourselves, or that others have constructed for us, is too small a container to hold what is waiting to emerge from within us. For many of us there are unspoken wishes, unfulfilled dreams or internal longings that we would never dare to acknowledge. If we were to pursue those parts of ourselves, what would other people think? What would other people say? What if people I care about won't understand? What if it can't work? How would the world possibly understand or make room for these deeper aspirations? After all, we live in a culture that doesn't usually honor our interior longings. Our family members, friends or co-workers might tell us we are dreaming, that life is not about dreams, that dreams are not the way life works. But what if dreams are exactly how life works? What if our dreams, our inner visions and images, our deepest urg-ings and desires, are exactly how life gets constructed? What if the naysayers are simply afraid to dream? What if our willingness to dream only reminds others of dreams forsaken? What if we all settle for dreams that are too small to contain our true essence?

---

*T*he movie version of *The Wizard of Oz* opens in black and white with Dorothy wandering the farm somewhat aimlessly and obviously disconnected from a sense of meaning and belonging in her life. While this Kansas farm may have been the safe womb of her childhood, it is no longer big enough to contain the next part of her story and we see her struggling with the rules, expectations and social constructs of her culture. The scenes are in black and white to represent the shadowy version of life we live in before we wake up to live more consciously from our deeper selves. Dorothy cannot live in color or out loud within the safe confines of her old structures and patterns. She has not yet taken her place in the center of her own story but rather is playing a bit part in a story that feels too small for her dreams and imaginations about life. She longs to be *somewhere over the rainbow,* in a place where she can breathe, sing and explore her true nature while following her intuition. It is at this point that Elvira Gulch comes in to take Toto, since he cannot be kept under control, and Dorothy is forced to flee the safety of the family farm and to follow her intuition as she takes those first frightful steps onto an unknown path.

Following the call of our intuition, the first steps on the hero's journey call us to question and examine our life vision. We often must renounce the life story given to us by family and external cultural expectations and begin earnestly seeking our own life guided by our inner visions and longings. Miss Gulch represents those rigid social and cultural constructs that become abhorrent to our developing sense of Self. Miss Gulch takes Toto as she symbolically attempts to separate Dorothy from her intuition in order to keep her under control. Like Dorothy, our early conditioning is often driven by family, social, cultural and religious structures designed to keep us safe but also to keep us under control. As we enter into our own story, we inevitably confront the structures and systems that will try to keep us where we are. But a part of us knows it is no longer enough to be safe, and it is no longer possible to stay under control. Some part of us knows that it is time to move beyond the safety of our old patterns and to begin following that part of us that longs for the freedom to experience the deeper and truer parts of ourselves. As we have recognized, Toto represents Dorothy's intuition. It is the work of our intuition to pull us into new places and even to create a disruption in our ordinary lives at times, in order to move us forward on the path of our hero's journey.

Desperate and confused, Dorothy looks for help only to realize that even those closest to her, Auntie Em and Uncle Henry, will not or cannot fight this battle for her. Auntie Em says to her, "we can't go against the law, Dorothy." The teaching of this stage of the journey is this: It is *our* story unfolding in front of us, and no one else can claim it for us. Our real duty, Campbell tells us, "is to go away from the community to find our bliss." This doesn't necessarily mean that we will literally leave the places and people in our lives.

More often it is a psychological leaving, a realignment of our awareness as we take our place as the hero of our own story. If we are to honor the deeper parts of us that are trying to emerge in our life, we must be willing to step into the leading role in our own story and to actively seek the life we find hidden in our dreams. We must take those first fateful steps onto an unknown path, willing to chart a course that is true to our soul. We must be willing to let go of the patterns that no longer serve us and follow our intuition, even if we are not sure of the destination.

In the chakra system this stage of the journey is connected to the first chakra. The first chakra represents the safety, security and survival conditioning of home, the family and the social order to which we belong. The first chakra is represented by the color red and the element of earth. It energetically resides in the base of our spine and is connected to the very roots of our spinal system and body. Metaphorically, the first chakra represents grounding in the physical world and the roots of our physical world learning about surviving and belonging from our early support structures. It is attached to our physical body, our physical home and our physical family. Carolyn Myss calls these early support structures *"the tribe"* and teaches that the work of the tribe is to keep us safe—but also to keep us in our place.

When we begin the hero's journey, we often hit the wall of the family or social rules we have been conditioned to follow. We are often conditioned to believe that there are no choices, that this is the way things are and that we need to learn to live within the boundaries of that reality. If we challenge the social order, the tribe generally does not applaud us or cheer us on. In fact, the family or culture will often swing into full force to keep us where we are and to stop any challenge to the constructed reality. The tribe does not want us to follow our intuition or our individual path. Individuation is a threat to the group consciousness. The tribe often ignites fear in the first chakra to keep us under control by telling us that it will not be safe if we stop following the tribal rules and that we will be left alone and vulnerable in the world. But when we begin to walk on our own path, we can no longer be controlled. The tribe comes in with the rules and the laws, the "shoulds" and the "should nots" and the fear messages intended to keep us where we are. We also must recognize that most of us have internalized these learned boundaries and beliefs and carry the tribal rules with us in our heads. Through these internalized messages we often imprison ourselves with these limitations whether there is a "tribe" around us or not.

The real challenge of the first chakra stage, however, is to take our place at the center of our own story. We are called to root ourselves in the clay or the earth of our own story. Irish priest, poet and philosopher John O'Donohue tells us that "our souls are artistically active in shaping forms of belonging in which we can truly rest, and from which our deepest possibilities can be challenged and awakened." Our inner voice calls us to create new forms of meaning and belonging, to establish new spiritual roots, which will nurture and support our newly awakening consciousness. As we begin to seek our true Self, we will all be called to make the first chakra choice to leave home, so to speak, and to create a new home and new roots in the spiritual world. When we begin to follow our inner voice, our intuition, we will be more difficult to control, because the world we have known becomes too small for us. We need to abandon the limitations of our old worldview and risk entering into a new world which is big enough for us to explore our deeper spiritual aspects and to emerge into the unique adventure that is our path.

Stepping Stones ◎◎◎

Awareness Affirmation: *I trust where my deeper urgings and awarenesses are leading me. I let go of patterns that limit or restrain my awakening sense of Self. I root myself in my own life story and embark with courage on a new path leading to deeper connection, meaning and purpose.*

What events that have recently occurred in your life resonate with this part of the journey?

◎ What parts of you, or of your life, have begun to feel uncomfortable, outgrown or limiting in some way?

◎ Are there places in your life that feel constricted, where it almost seems hard to breathe?

◎ Where in your life do you meet with resistance to expressing more of yourself or making changes?

◎ What family or social rules feel oppressive or onerous to you?

◎ What are the most significant fears that you are experiencing right now in your life?

◎ Who are the people in your life who are trying to keep you under control?

◎ How are you trying to keep yourself under control?

◎ What are the fear messages, the "shoulds," or the "should nots," that stop you from taking the next steps?

Withdrawal

"*Detachment or Withdrawal ... Consists of a Radical Transfer of Emphasis from the External to the Internal World*"

~ JOSEPH CAMPBELL

Once we answer the call and begin to take our leave from our old familiar patterns and constructs, we are swept out of the external world and pulled deep into the waters of our inner world. We begin whirling in our own unconscious, exploring through our inner dreams and images the seeds of our life that are waiting to be uncovered. This inner world is filled not only with our secret longings and passions, however, but with parts of ourselves that we have ignored or pushed away. It is where we stuffed our feelings of grief, anger, disappointment, abandonment or betrayal. It is where we buried parts of ourselves that have not been honored by our families, friends, teachers or partners. It is where we stored the life crises, losses and traumas that separated us from our hopes and our dreams. This inner world is a memorial to the myriad ways we have been dis-membered by the events of our lives. When we enter this world, we must be prepared to re-member and reclaim our lost parts and to tease our hopes and dreams away from the terrors and traumas that seemingly interrupted our magnificent stories. We must make peace with our past and with the people who played a role in the drama of our life story. This inner work is the stuff that most people push away for one reason or another—too busy, too scary, too painful, too needy, too much. *But if we wish to reclaim our deepest parts, if we wish to re-member who we really are, we must begin within. When we gather the courage and the fortitude to open the door to this inner world, a threshold is passed, God walks in with us, and nothing will ever be the same again.*

---

*W*hen Dorothy decides to leave the old patterns behind and take the next steps on her journey, she first meets the magician who she hopes will help her to escape her past and to see her future. Instead, like a good therapist, he cleverly directs her back to the place where her life began, that gray and quiet Kansas farm, where she must begin her journey into the inner world. But as she returns to her childhood home, she is confronted with the full force of the cyclone that very literally sweeps her out of her external world and into the Land of Oz. The cyclone turns her familiar world around and around, picking up her childhood house and dropping her in Oz. By the disorienting power and force of the cyclone, Dorothy's home is metaphorically moved from her outer world to her inner world. As Dorothy emerges in the land of Oz, she discovers a magical place that is rich with color and images, as well as strange and fantastical characters and occurrences. As Dorothy peers out into this magical land, she intuitively knows that an important threshold has been crossed. Dorothy declares, "Toto, I have a feeling we're not in Kansas any more!"

When we venture outside the safety of our ordinary reality and take our first steps toward our true Self, the

Universe shows up to meet us—sometimes in the form of a friendly magician who kindly guides us along our way, and sometimes with the full force of a cyclone that disorients us and turns our world upside down. We often begin our journey like Dorothy trying to escape from our past or to run from our troubles. If we are lucky, a friendly magician, a good friend or a wise therapist will remind us that we cannot outrun our inner life and that escape isn't really an option. Our hero's journey most often begins right in the middle of our ordinary life where eventually our intuition leads us to the threshold of our inner world, inviting us to sort through our troubles and traumas on our way to discovering the truth of who we are.

Like Dorothy entering the Land of Oz, most of us find the inner world a strange and unfamiliar place. Its images, metaphors and symbols are often unfamiliar, confusing and disorienting. We've spent our lives looking outside for answers, reacting and responding to the "reality" of the outer world, attempting to solve our problems by adapting, adjusting and acquiescing to the demands from outside of ourselves. When we are pulled into our inner world, it can feel as unfamiliar as the mythical Land of Oz, and we begin to wonder what is real as we spin through old stories and as our footholds in the ordinary world are stripped away.

Dorothy's journey to the inner world begins inside her home in the eye of a cyclone with the images from her outer life and her inner life spinning curiously and confusingly around her. When she lands, she steps out into a strange and unfamiliar world. Crossing that threshold from our external world into our inner world can feel exciting, terrifying or, as is usually the case, both at the same time. Initially it creates a feeling of being disoriented, of walking in a strange yet alluring land where we don't know the landmarks. Campbell tells us that it is here where we will find all of the ogres and secret helpers of our childhood. But once we cross that threshold we know, as Dorothy knew, that we can't go back the way we came, so we hesitantly move along this new path feeling ungrounded and off balance, needing to find our way in this mysterious inner world.

As frightening as it may seem to dive into the waters of the inner world, however, there is no path into our intended life story that can bypass the road through our past and through our own unconscious. Like Dorothy, we have to be willing to wander through this strange and uncomfortable territory if we want to find our way home. Gratefully, the myths teach us that if we choose to move toward our deepest Self, the forces of the Universe will conspire to help us. The Gospel of James promises, "Draw near to him and he will draw near to you" (James 4:8). If we will take the first steps in our inner world, we can depend on our intuition, our inner imagination and the inherent wisdom of the Universe to meet us at that threshold and to guide the way.

In the chakra system as we move out of the first chakra, the social and family structures of our external world, we enter the internal world of our second chakra. The second chakra is represented by the color orange and the element of water. The second chakra is located in our pelvis. It is in the second chakra where we find a flowing and moving sense of passion and vital energy for life. The second chakra is also where we record and store our feelings about the people and events of our past. It is where we hold the energy of our relationships with other people in our lives and where our past experiences leave stories of good and evil, right and wrong, pleasure and pain, victims and villains. These shadows of our past often unconsciously drive the patterns and choices of our present, and unless and until we resolve these old stories and emotional traumas, we may find ourselves reliving these old patterns over and over in our outer world. The people may change, but the patterns remain.

The work of this second chakra stage of our journey is to sort through the old stories and experiences of our past and decide if we still want them to define us. Often these old stories in our second chakra become the scripts we use to engage with people in our outer life, unconsciously directing how we feel about ourselves and how we engage in our relationships with others. For example, if we have second chakra experiences of being victimized in our early life, we will often find ourselves repeating the victim pattern over and over with people in our life. If we have experiences of being the rescuer in our family of origin, we will search for people in our life who need to be rescued. If we were abandoned or betrayed by people we loved, we may unconsciously engage in relationships that result in experiences of abandonment or betrayal. The lesson of the second chakra is that if we get stuck in unconscious emotional reactions to old stories and traumas, we will spend our days repeatedly engaged in dramas filled with struggle and conflict, rather than going inside and doing the inner sorting work that is really the call of this stage.

Parker Palmer describes this dilemma of the second chakra by saying, "if we do not understand that the enemy is within, we will find a thousand ways of making someone 'out there' into the enemy." As Dorothy enters Oz, the Wicked Witch bursts onto the scene in a red pillar of smoke, bearing a striking resemblance to a figure from her past. Buried in Dorothy's second chakra is the witch of her past, Elvira Gulch. She shows up in red smoke, representing the fear of the first chakra, and makes clear her intention to keep Dorothy a prisoner of her fears and projections. But once we enter our inner world, we have to decide what's real. We have to decide that whatever is happening in our external world is giving us clues about our internal world. Most of the people or situations that disturb us on the outside are shadowy projections of the darker places or stories inside of us. We can focus on the witch outside of ourselves, or we can go inside, clean our emotional closets and do our inner work to heal the traumas of our past. It is through this second chakra cleaning work that we make room for new and more expansive possibilities in our future.

The inner work of the second chakra is to use our feelings to make peace with the people and experiences of our past, knowing that they were playing a role in a drama that was designed to bring forward our highest potential. Whatever we reject, whatever we push away, whatever we do not want to face, will find a way to show up in our life again and again in various forms and uncomfortable ways until we work through it and include it as a learning experience along our journey. In Dorothy's story we can easily see the projection of Elvira Gulch onto the Wicked Witch of the West, the central character of Dorothy's struggle in Oz. Dorothy thinks she can run away from Gulch, but her nemesis is just transformed into a more fearsome witch. We all have witches, demons and fearsome creatures in our history, and sometimes we are pulled into our depths before being called to our heights. But the teaching of the second chakra is to face and confront our inner stories about the people and experiences on the path we have walked— the good and the bad, the pleasant and the painful, the victims and the villains—and ultimately to honor them all as necessary to our full unfolding into the mystery of our lives. Sometimes it takes a scary witch to help us find our courage or to push us onto our "yellow brick road." If Elvira Gulch does not enter onto the scene of her life, Dorothy stays in Kansas, dreaming about the land "somewhere over the rainbow," rather than stepping into her own hero's adventure and ultimately seeking and finding the mystery of her being.

The wisdom of the second chakra is to remember that it is not the events of our life but how we hold and story them that gives them the power to keep us from our highest Self. The second chakra is our emotional center where we use our feelings to guide us along our journey. When we are connected to the flow of our feelings, they easily and gently guide us toward the people and experiences that serve us and away from those that do not. But if we store up too much emotional trauma in the second chakra without consciously sorting through the feelings, we can drown in our old stories. If we dam up our feeling senses to avoid our anger, sadness or pain, our life can feel dried up and depressed. But if we honor our feelings and work with the messages they bring forward, they will provide the passion and the current to move us toward our highest Self. The surface wants and desires of our small self will give way to the deeper aspirations of our spiritual Self. If we are willing to do the shadow and consciousness work of the second chakra, life takes on a feeling of flowing water, a moving story where we no longer get stopped, instead of a feeling of drowning in the watery darkness of the old stories.

Stepping Stones ◎ ◎ ◎

Awareness Affirmation: *I face my past without fear, shame, guilt or regret. I honor the parts of myself that have felt sad, confused, angry or afraid and let go of patterns that no longer serve me. I am safe to explore my inner world, to integrate all of my lost parts and to reclaim my passion for life.*

What events that have recently occurred in your life resonate with this part of the journey?

◎ What does it feel like when you go into your inner world?

◎ What images and stories show up in your dreams and unconscious images?

◎ What buried feelings, old wounds or painful stories are you holding in your second chakra?

◎ Is there anger, sadness, fear, loneliness, anxiety, depression or a sense of heaviness?

◎ Can you journal about these feelings and let the experiences come into consciousness?

◎ How have you learned to avoid these feelings rather than work with them and through them?

◎ Do you have a recurring "wicked witch" story that keeps showing up in your life, making you feel small and afraid? Name the people who have played this role in your life. How have they stopped you or pushed you along your path?

◉ How are you holding or storying your life events in ways
   that keep you feeling powerless, or afraid to move forward?

◉ Who would you have to release, let go of or forgive to
   move forward?

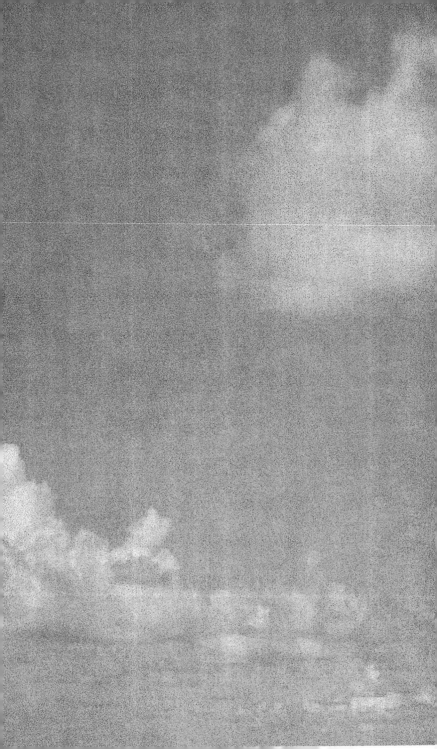

We Begin Alone

"Where There Is a Way or a Path, It Is Someone Else's Way.
Each Knight Enters the Forest at the Most Mysterious Point
and Follows His Own Intuition."

~ JOSEPH CAMPBELL

The myths of the West remind us that the knight always had to begin his journey alone. Where there was a well-trodden path or others to follow, it inevitably led to the hero's death. The teaching in the East is that you must swim in your own river or die. As we commit ourselves to walk the hero's journey, we must chart our own way. We must remember who we are and set off on the path that only our soul can perceive. When we really commit to walk into our own stories—to leave the well-worn path and to close out the clamor of the external world—we often feel as though we've walked into a dark alley permeated by an eerie silence. Our first impulse is to find a brightly lit highway and follow anything that moves in an attempt to reorient ourselves and to feel connected to something familiar. Following the bright lights and the voices that shout from outside "Go this way" or "Go that way" feels like the smart move when we're alone, afraid and unsure. But the connection that truly keeps us safe is the connection to our deeper Self, to our soul, to the small inner voice that says, "Go your way." This voice whispers to us in the dark, "don't be afraid, this is the way, trust your Self." This voice tells us to just start walking from where we are. This voice reminds

*us that there is a mystery unfolding in front of us that we cannot
see. This voice reminds us that we can never be lost when we follow
our soul. This voice reminds us that we are always connected to the
very source of our being, and we are never alone.*

After Dorothy lands in Oz and meets the munchkins that live there, Glinda, the Good Witch of the North, floats in on a beautiful pink bubble. She thanks Dorothy for killing the Wicked Witch of the East and magically places the ruby slippers upon Dorothy's feet. When the Wicked Witch of the West arrives and threatens to harm Dorothy, she discovers that Dorothy is wearing the ruby slippers. Glinda tells the Wicked Witch, "You have no power here. Begone." Glinda warns Dorothy never to remove the ruby slippers from her feet, for that would put her at the Witch's mercy. When Dorothy asks how to find her way home, she is directed to the Great Wizard of Oz in the Emerald City for assistance. Dorothy asks Glinda how she will get to the Emerald City and is told that she must walk. She asks where to begin and is told that the best place to begin is at the beginning, and her attention is drawn to a path beginning under the ruby slippers on her feet. Unwinding in a golden spiral in front of Dorothy is the beginning of the yellow brick road to Oz.

The two primary symbols of the Oz story are introduced in this stage of the journey: the ruby slippers and the yellow brick road. The ruby slippers represent our connection to our soul. The yellow brick road represents the spiral path of consciousness that we all travel. As we journey with Dorothy into this next stage of her journey, Glinda arrives as a beautiful pink figure representing the power of love and compassion. The Wicked Witch of the West bursts in on a plume of fire and red smoke and represents the smaller part of our nature that is ruled by fear and foreboding. Glinda reminds us that if we can be present to ourselves with true love and compassion, fear has no power over us and we are safe to continue our journey into our inner world. As we have learned, the inner world of our second chakra contains the seeds of trauma, loss, grief and disappointment over our early life experiences, and the fear of further trauma can certainly stop us in our tracks. But Glinda places the ruby slippers on Dorothy's feet as a symbol of her connection with her soul. When Dorothy connects with her soul, she begins to walk the path that will lead her out of the trauma of her human experiences and into the deeper possibilities of her true Self. One of the clear teachings of this myth is that only with love and compassion for ourselves can we really begin to walk into our soul's truest expression.

The heroic myths of old teach that we each have our own path to walk in the world and that we must begin that walk alone. In the ancient myths the knight always entered onto the path alone and in the darkest place. A true hero was never able to follow the path of another journeyer, for that would mean sure and certain death. We find this theme of beginning mythic journeys alone and uncertain in classic and modern literature. Dante begins the classic *Commedia* with the words, "In the middle of the road of my life I awoke in a dark wood, where the way was truly lost." And when we are lost and alone in the dark, we all ask, as Dorothy does, where do we begin? In his book *The Heart Aroused*, author and poet David Whyte tells us that "the journey begins right here. In the middle of the road. Right beneath your feet. This is the place. There is no other place and no other time." As frightening and confusing as the unseen future may seem at times, the only place to begin our own story is indeed at the beginning, placing one foot in front of the other and walking, step by step, stage by stage through the uncomfortable and the uncertain, sure only of the inevitability of the journey.

In the Oz story, Glinda and the munchkins can wish Dorothy well and cheer her on as she begins her journey to find the Wizard of Oz, but no one can accompany her into her inner world, for that is a journey she must begin alone, aided only by her intuition, Toto. Moreover, Dorothy could not be magically transported to the Great and Powerful Oz, because we come into our spiritual awareness as we walk the path of consciousness, step by step and stage by stage. Spiritual unfolding is a developmental process, not a magical moment. We must be patient as Spirit unfolds a path in front of us and remain willing to follow the path without turning back. Trust, patience and perseverance are characteristics of the spiritual journeyer. If we can accept life as a journey with an unknown destination, if we can stay connected with our soul and learn to trust the process of life, if we are willing each day to put one foot in front of the other, then the path will unfold in front of us just like the yellow brick road.

The first steps of Dorothy's journey to Oz begin on a winding yellow brick road representing the development of consciousness along a spiral path. Carl Jung teaches that although we may seem to come around and around in life, sometimes repeating the same types of experiences and dramas, we are not traveling in circles. Rather, we are traveling on a spiral path, slowly deepening in our understanding of ourselves and our place in the universe. If we consciously walk the spiral path, we can approach the journey of life with focus and awareness, and through each experience of life we will learn more and more about ourselves and about the journey of consciousness we are all embarked upon. As we become more and more conscious, we expand in our ability to know ourselves and to move more consistently from our knowledge of the deep and essential truth of who we are. This is the spiral path of evolution.

As we walk the spiral path we must follow the advice that Glinda gives Dorothy and never remove our ruby slippers. The ruby slippers are our reminder that we are always connected to our souls and will be guided by our intuition and held in a divine flow of love and compassion. We must remember that as we walk through the confusion, struggles and hardships of life, we are always protected by our connection to our souls. Just as the Wicked Witch is powerless over Dorothy when she is connected to the ruby slippers and in the presence of the love and compassion of Glinda, if we follow our intuition and stay in connection with our soul, the external world will hold no power over us and we can walk through our fears unharmed. When we feel separate from our soul, ignore our intuition, lose our sense of compassion and forget that we are always connected to the divine, a sense of fear and foreboding about life can overtake us and create a prison that keeps us from expressing our deepest truth.

This stage of the journey represents the third chakra of the eastern system. The third chakra is yellow and is represented by the element of fire. The third chakra is located in the solar plexus. The third chakra is where we find the fire of our personal power and begin to walk in the integrity of who we are. The third chakra is where we begin to individuate from our families and friends and experience our sense of personal power. We know we are in the strength of the third chakra when we stand tall and supported from the center of our body. We know we are being challenged in our third chakra when we fold our arms over the center of our body and close ourselves off in a protective stance. All the *self* words reside in the third chakra—self-confident, self-sufficient, self-reliant, self-supporting, self-determined, and yes, self-doubt.

The work of the third chakra is to find our focus—holding our intention firmly in mind in the presence of the world's distractions. We must focus on the path before us and walk forward alone, shutting out the clamor, control and conditioning of our past and of the external world. We must focus on our own stories. We must start to think for ourselves and know for ourselves. Being able to hold one's focus and intention firmly in mind in the chaos and confusion of the world is a mark of spiritual maturity.

When we begin the work of the third chakra we are called to reexamine everything we have been taught to believe about our life and its meaning. The third chakra is where we hold our organizing thoughts and beliefs about the world and, most importantly, about ourselves. As Dorothy begins her walk down the yellow brick road, she notices that things are very different from what they were in Kansas; talking scarecrows and angry apple trees remind her that she is not in Kansas any more, and she is called to reexamine her organizing assumptions about how life works. As we begin our third chakra work, we must examine our old beliefs about the world and be prepared to see the world with new eyes. We have to question what we've been told, what we thought we knew and what "everyone knows" to be true, and begin to see things from a new perspective. We have to let go of the "Kansas" of collective consciousness and bring our deeper awareness into focus on the truth about ourselves, our lives and our journey.

When we begin to examine and question our conditioned thoughts and beliefs, we really begin our own adventure—on our own feet, on our own path, from our own center. This is where we begin to stand in the integrity of who we are and begin to practice strategically seeing the course in front of us with awareness and consciousness. This is where we use the fire of our intention to burn away the thoughts and stories that no longer serve us and to forge a path where none seems obvious. This is where we begin to emerge as the hero in our own story.

Stepping Stones ◎ ◎ ◎ ◎

Awareness Affirmation: *I stand with strength in the light of my soul and believe in my power to walk the path of consciousness. I hold myself with love and compassion as I move more deeply toward the center of my being with focus and confidence.*

_____

What events that have recently occurred in your life resonate with this part of the journey?

◎ Can you remember a time in your life when you had the feeling of being alone, in the dark, yet knowing you must begin to walk?

◎ Where in your life do you have the feeling that a path is opening before you? What thoughts arise as you contemplate beginning to walk that path?

◎ Have you tried following others on their pre-existing and well-trodden paths and been stopped?

◎ Where do the voices of fear and self-doubt come from, and what do they say to stop you or discourage you from moving forward?

◎ If you pay attention to your thoughts do you notice repetative negative or limiting thoughts?

◎ How might these negative thoughts be shaping your outer experiences?

◎ What beliefs about the world do you find yourself challenging or reexamining?

◎ What new insights are you beginning to have about who you are?

◎ What new "truths" about life are beginning to take form in your consciousness?

Guides and Threshold Guardians

"As You Now Go Towards the Center,
There Will Come More Aids,
as Well as Increasingly Difficult Trials."

~ JOSEPH CAMPBELL

As we make the commitment to take the hero's journey, to step across that threshold and onto our path, we are sure to be met by the threshold guardians. Threshold guardians are the gargoyles and creatures that appear on the path to test our resolve and to turn back the faint of heart. As we begin to walk in our own story we will find these guardians standing tall along the way, revealing our tightly held fears, insecurities and attachments. They will come in the form of obstacles, delays and detours. They will come in the voices of those around us who say it can't be done. They will come in our inner voices that tell us there is not enough time, not enough money, not enough support or not the right conditions to allow us to move forward. Worst of all they will come in the form of voices from inside or outside to tell us that we are not enough somehow to be worthy of our dreams. But the myths also promise that if we commit to our own true adventure, magical guides will appear to help and doors will open only for us. On the other side of every obstacle before us is the opportunity to move more deeply into the center of our story. Our life dreams await us, and angelic helpers conspire with us to bring them forward. So as we are faced with the threshold guardians, we must keep walking. If we get stopped, we must ask for help and look for it to appear. No cry for help goes unanswered—we just sometimes miss the disguises of the helpers. When a stranger offers a new perspective, when a family member whispers "good for you," when a mentor or teacher recognizes our gifts, these are the helpers moving us forward on the path that lies before us.

$\mathcal{A}$s Dorothy begins her walk down the yellow brick road, the Wicked Witch promises, "I'll get you, my pretty, and your little dog too." Lurking behind trees and around dark corners, the Witch lies in wait for the opportunity to stop Dorothy on her journey. Threshold guardians show up in the form of talking apple trees, in worries of "lions and tigers and bears, oh my," in fields of intoxicating poppies and in the winged monkeys and fearsome creatures of the dark forest. But also watching the way is Glinda, the Good Witch, and she always seems to respond when the call for help goes out.

The stories we tell ourselves have the power to imprison us or to liberate us. If we tell ourselves we are all alone and create stories filled with darkness, danger and terror, we will create lives that are too small, built on safety and protection, void of the opportunities to live our dreams and to discover who we really are. Part of our work on the hero's journey is to create stories for ourselves that are big enough to hold the deep mystery of who we are and the vast possibilities that lie beneath the surface of our ordinary lives.

The paradox for all of us in this process is that stories that are too big overwhelm us and can be as disempowering as stories that are too small. When we reach for dreams that are too far from our current reality, it is hard for us to believe those dreams are possible and the barriers that stand in front of us seem insurmountable. The trick of the hero's journey is to take one stage of the path at a time, knowing that there will be challenges and obstacles at each stage, yet trusting that all we need to continue will be provided if we stay true to ourselves.

Huston Smith, the great scholar and teacher of world religions, likes the prayer "let gentle light." He teaches that this prayer asks for just enough light to take the next step on the journey, for if we could see all the way to the end of our lives, many of us would not venture to take the first step. If we can learn to take life one step at a time, staying present in the moment and asking for just enough light for each day, we will find the courage to venture into the unknown but ever-present possibilities of our lives.

The myths tell us that the closer we get to our deeper Selves, the more challenges we will face. These challenges are the threshold guardians along the path. The threshold guardians are represented in medieval architecture as the gargoyles and creatures at the gates of the great cathedrals and in medieval stories as trolls under bridges. In life the threshold guardians show up in the form of obstacles, naysayers and fear mongers. They are the voices in our heads or the voices of those around us that tell us not to venture, not to risk, not to seek, not to dream. They try to lull us back into the old ways, the old patterns and the old structures that have supported our lives. The test of our third chakra strength is to push through these obstacles with the certainty of our connection to Self and the guidance of our intuition; these obstacles, the threshold guardians, challenge us to release all that is false and to acknowledge the soul of who we are. They come to test our resolve, our fortitude, our focus and our perseverance. These qualities are the pearls of the third chakra work, and we will be given many opportunities to test and fortify these hard-earned strengths.

On the brighter side, as we stand firm in our resolve to walk our path, the Universe lines up to support us. Guidance always comes, often in forms unexpected, sometimes friendly and sometimes fearsome. Guidance may show up in the form of the munchkins, the friendly presences that cheer us on our way and joyfully point us in the right direction—or in beautiful pink bubbles filled with love and compassion appearing at just the right moment—or in the form of scarecrows, tin men or lions that become our loyal companions along the way—or in the form of a Miss Gulch or a witch, the ominous presences that press us forward even when we are not sure we are really ready to go.

The myths promise that as we make our way through the confusion and challenges of our journey, help is always available. In the Oz story, our heroine and her companions show us that just when all seems lost, a good cry for help will bring forward exactly the assistance that is needed. Just as Glinda's soft light floats ever present in the background of the Oz journey, watching over our heroine as she makes her way, that "gentle light" Smith prays for will come if we soften our fear and remember our connection to All That Is. When we connect deeply with our deepest Self, we also connect with something immensely bigger than ourselves—we connect with an unseen presence that holds within it all of our deepest possibilities as well as the pathways to get there.

We must remember to ask for help, however, and we must recognize the helpers as they appear: a nudge by a friend toward something we missed; an intuition that causes us to turn or act at just the right time; the uncanny coincidences and synchronicities that direct us to just the right place at just the right time with just the right people. Startlingly, the more we listen and the more we pay attention, the more help we seem to receive. Whether ghoulish or gracious, as we move along the path we somehow begin to trust that there will always be help. As Campbell describes, when we follow our hero's journey and open more and more deeply to ourselves, doors and opportunities begin to open in front of us that would not have opened for anyone else. This is the magic of the path. When we are truly on our own adventure, life begins to open up before us and we find ourselves in a synchronistic flow of guidance and support.

As we allow ourselves to be present to this deeper flow in our lives, we learn to look beyond the experiences and challenges we encounter and to see life as an invitation to come into deeper awareness of our true Self. Some experiences will invite us to drop the false exteriors we have created for safety and acceptance. Some experiences will challenge us to reach deep within ourselves for gifts, strengths and abilities we didn't know we had. The presence of challenges and struggles in life are sure signs that we are being invited to learn more about who we really are and to face and surrender the fears, emotions and beliefs that no longer serve us. At this stage of the journey the hero begins to trust that we are never alone and that all experiences in life are meaningful opportunities to learn and grow. We stop looking for the answers to life outside of us and begin to accept our deeper intuitions and knowings as we move forward on our path. This represents a fundamental shift in our consciousness, which opens and expands our capacity to be present to the mystery of life unfolding through us and around us.

Stepping Stones

Awareness Affirmation: *I stay open to the mystery of life unfolding before me. I face the challenges of life with confidence, perseverance and focus. Every experience is an invitation to discover the truth of who I am. I receive help and support in expected and unexpected ways.*

What events that have recently occurred in your life resonate with this part of the journey?

◎ Where in your life do you confront the threshold guardians?

◎ What are their voices saying to you?

◎ How do they try to distract you or to interrupt your journey?

◎ What are the old fears or stories that can be triggered by the threshold guardians?

◎ How is guidance appearing in your life?

◎ Who are the helpers you have encountered along your path?

◎ Can you name both friends and foes who have helped you learn more about yourself?

◎ How do you know when guidance is operating?

◎ How does your intuition communicate with you to give you guidance?

Totems of the Path

"When You Reach the Upper Chakras, You Don't Do without the First Three. You Don't Destroy the First Three Floors of a Building When You Get to the Fourth."

~ JOSEPH CAMPBELL

The beginning legs of the spiritual path can be difficult and exhausting, but the struggles of these first three stages are the foundational blocks that will support our progress as we continue on our path. In the eastern spiritual traditions the first three chakras represent our "lower nature," our human experiences and aspects, our physical, emotional and mental bodies. As we work with the first three chakras, we face our fears, explore our emotional stories and confront the thoughts and beliefs that control the way we see ourselves and the world. Metaphorically we clean the closets of our past and prepare to move forward with a lighter load and with more of our energy available for the journey.

As we move along the path of spiritual development, the lower chakras bring with them two common hazards. The first comes in our refusal to honestly do our work with these parts of ourselves. There is a tendency to race toward the end of the spiritual journey—seeking the promise of peace, joy and bliss—without uncovering and healing the shadow parts of our personalities. We avoid the anxieties and fears, the negative emotions and the disempowering beliefs of these centers, because they challenge us to touch the wounds and traumas of our past and do the hard work of forgiveness and healing. Unfortunately, the unhealed stories and patterns of our past will continue to create havoc and distractions for us as we try to follow our spiritual path. Until we deal with the sorrows, shames and shadows of our past experiences, we will inevitably find ourselves back in old patterns and relationships, repeating lessons we thought we had learned.

The second danger in following the spiritual path is to cut ourselves off from our lower centers in a desire to live the "spiritual life." We deny our physical needs or realities, we repress our deep emotional responses and we forego the objective and rational thinking that allows us to function effectively on the planet. We can fill our days with ascetic physical practices, elaborate and emotional rituals or fantastical and magical thinking about all things spiritual. In the process we actually become cut off from ourselves, from others and from the world. Those who have struggled with addictions in the physical world may find that they have simply exchanged their worldly addictive patterns for "spiritually" addictive patterns.

We must remember that we came to the planet in human form—with a body, with feelings and with a reasoning mind. These are the gifts of being in human form: our sensations, our passions, our need for relationships and our capacity to explore, learn and evolve through all that we experience. These are the rich experiences that make us human and that provide us with opportunities to grow and evlove in our awareness and consciousness as we move along our path. We cannot ignore these parts of ourselves, nor can we abandon them in search of our higher self. The spiritual work of our lower chakras is to clear out the old stories, traumas and patterns that limit our development and then consciously integrate the lessons so that we can use the powers of these chakras in service to the awakening Self.

*A*s Dorothy emerges from the third stage of her journey, she has walked through the challenges of the first three chakras and is now accompanied by three faithful companions as totems of her inner work—the Lion, the Tin Man and the Scarecrow. These three companions represent the three energy centers of our lower nature, the first three chakras of the eastern system. Each of these chakra centers has a power or strength, as well as a shadow or vulnerability. Dorothy's three companions clearly illustrate both the power and the peril of each of these chakras.

Courage vs. Fear

The Lion represents the first chakra. The first chakra power is the energy of courage that allows us to stand and take our place as "King of the Forest" or the hero in the center of our own adventure. The shadow side of the first chakra is fear. Before the Lion aligns with Dorothy on her soul walk, he is paralyzed with fears and unable to function. The Lion is startled by anything that moves and worries that all of the forest creatures are laughing at him. The Lion cannot possibly take his place as King of the Forest because his fears and insecurities stop him at every turn.

In the Oz story when the Lion asks him for courage, the Wizard says to the Lion, "You have plenty of courage, I am sure. All you need is confidence in yourself. There is no living thing that is not afraid when it faces danger. True courage is in facing danger when you are afraid, and that kind of courage you have in plenty." When the Lion learns to own his internal sense of power, he finds that his instincts serve him well to warn him when danger is present, and his courage allows him to handle those situations with confidence. A healthy first chakra provides us with the common sense and grounding we need to effectively navigate the physical world and the courage to keep moving forward even in the face of adversity.

The symbol of the lion reminds us that it takes courage to leave the old life patterns behind and to walk the hero's path before us in spite of our fears and in spite of what other people may think about us. Campbell says, "It takes courage to do what you want. Other people have a lot of plans for you. Nobody wants you to do what you want to do. They want you to go on their trip, but you can do what you want." The lion energy of the first chakra reminds us that life is not for cowards. If we decide to walk into our own story, challenges and struggles will appear along the path, and plenty of naysayers will line up along the way. The lion calls us to have the courage to stand firmly on the earth, rooted in our own story, and walk through the shadows and dark forests of life to fulfill our life purpose.

Passion vs. Purgatory

The Tin Man represents the emotional energy of our second chakra—our feeling center. The second chakra power is the home of our passion for life. Our passions and feelings are part of our internal guidance system and are critical to our success in walking our path. But the Tin Man also shows us the shadow side of the second chakra—the danger of getting overwhelmed and paralyzed by our emotions. The second chakra is where we have stored all of our past emotional disappointments, wounds and traumas with other people. If we get lost in these old stories, we create a purgatory in our second chakra where we repetitively relive the emotional patterns of our past and find ourselves unable to find the path out of them. We become locked up like the Tin Man, paralyzed and stuck in the grip of our disempowering emotions.

The other danger of the second chakra is the tendency at this stage of our evolution to see life in dualities. In the land of the second chakra things tend to be good or evil, right or wrong, pleasant or painful. The second chakra sees life in black and white with no shades of gray. As Campbell says, "it is the land of ogres and fairy godmothers, with little in between." One of the spiritual requirements of walking the hero's journey, however, is to begin to see the paradox in all things. The Oz myth certainly teaches us that things are not always as they appear. In a world where paradox is the rule, we have to pause as we reflect on the experiences of life and seek for the meaning behind the madness.

As our heroine makes her way through Oz, she will find that a deeper look into the nature of things reveals the light behind the darkness and the truth beyond the illusion. The Wizard is both mystic and magician, the Witch's power is both wicked and weak, the ominous guards are both foe and friend. Twentieth century psychiatrist Carl Jung teaches us that everything in the world is made up of light and shadow. The Kabbalist mystics of the Judaic tradition teach that in every experience, interaction and person, a holy spark of the divine is always waiting to be pulled from the shadows. As we grow in our spiritual wisdom, we must become wary of the dualistic judgments that come forward from the second chakra and avoid the oversimplification of seeing things in black and white. We have to remember Dorothy's awareness that "we're not in Kansas anymore" as she leaves the black and white world of her childhood farm and discovers the colorful world of magic and mystery in Oz. We must learn to look behind the surface for the spark of light and divinity hidden in all of our experiences and in all of the people that we meet along our path.

The power of the second chakra is our passion—our vital life energy. When we are able to harness the passion of the second chakra, we use our feelings for guidance and for inner awareness. We need our feeling senses flowing like water without carrying us away in a tide of uncontrolled emotions or without getting dammed up in murky, sludgy pools of past sorrows or disappointments. If we become stuck in time in the insults, injuries and stories of the past or in dualistic judgments about the events of our life or the people on our path, we will not be able to move forward on the hero's journey.

The Wizard tells the Tin Man that he is "wrong to want a heart, as it makes most people unhappy." In the Oz story the Tin Man is indeed found rigid and motionless, paralyzed by the tears and experiences of his past. But having a heart or having an open heart is not what causes pain and unhappiness. Like the Tin Man, many people live an unhappy life because they get emotionally stuck in their old stories and traumas. Their inability to heal and move forward stops them from laying claim to their passion as the fuel for their spiritual evolution. As Dorothy oils and lubricates his joints, paying attention to all the frozen parts, the Tin Man re-enters the flow of life and is able to walk the yellow brick road of his journey. He learns to manage his emotions while keeping his heart open. Likewise, we must pay attention to the rigid and frozen stories in our past and spend time loosening and lubricating our old wounds. Healing our past will help us to harness the passion of the second chakra and to avoid the purgatory of emotional stories and traumas that stop us from moving fluidly and flexibly though our life journey.

Focus vs. Firestorm

The Scarecrow represents the mental energy of the third chakra. The power of the third chakra is the focus we find when we use this strategic, rational thinking center that helps us problem-solve along the path. Just as the second chakra is an emotional storehouse of our past experiences, the strategic mind of the third chakra is a mental storehouse of our past experiences. It represents acquired knowledge and mental patterns gained through life experience. The rational mind can be a tremendous tool as we negotiate our way along the path. The Wizard says to the Scarecrow when he asks for brains, "You don't need them. You learn something every day. A baby has brains but it doesn't know much. Experience is the only thing that brings knowledge, and the longer you are on earth, the more experience you are sure to get."

Likewise, our journey along the path of life helps us gain needed knowledge and experience in the world. But the worldly knowledge of the third chakra is of no use unless it acts in service to our intuition and spiritual wisdom. When Dorothy meets the Scarecrow at her first crossroads on the way to Oz, he spins himself into circles saying, "You could go this way, you could go that way, many go this way." Left on its own, our strategic mind will leave us confused and spinning in circles with its mental gymnastics, weighing options and seeking solutions to problems without even understanding the mystery unfolding in front of us. The strategic mind is not equipped to see with wisdom or vision. Those are capacities of our inner eye or of our higher mind. Einstein called this higher mind our "intuitive mind" and wrote that "the intuitive mind is a sacred gift and the rational mind is a faithful servant. We have created a society that honors the servant and has forgotten the gift." The Scarecrow wisely acknowledges the proper place of brains in the order of things when he declares to Dorothy as he joins her on her path that "I won't try to manage things." The Scarecrow, representing the third chakra, is wise to know that on the journey through our inner world to our spiritual consciousness, the strategic or rational mind can serve as a problem solver but must defer to the wisdom of the higher spiritual energies and follow the intuitive mind on the path of the soul.

The shadow side of the third chakra is the firestorm of thoughts, ideas and beliefs that can paralyze us as surely as the Lion's fears or the Tin Man's tears. The Scarecrow's greatest terror is fire, but fire represents both the power and the shadow of the third chakra. When we use the power of the third chakra as a strategic problem solver, it helps us find the fiery focus we need to chart the way on our path with grit and determination. When we let the shadow of the third chakra get in charge, however, it can create a firestorm of self-defeating mental patterns and contradicting thoughts and beliefs that will burn us up along with our dreams. Remember that the gift of the rational mind is to take things apart and break them down into pieces that can be logically analyzed. If we turn that atomizing mind loose to make sense of our spiritual journey, it will break us down and tear us apart with confusion, insecurity and self-doubt, the way the Scarecrow is torn apart by the winged monkeys, or it will set our small minds on fire with fear the way the Wicked Witch hurls fireballs at the Scarecrow in the dark forest.

Again, we must remember that the path to our soul is through the higher mind, following our intuition. Our rational or strategic mind can become an obstacle to our spiritual development because it cannot understand or make sense of this higher way of knowing. Huston Smith, preeminent synthesizer and teacher of world religions, compares the strategic mind trying to understand soul consciousness to a dog trying to make sense of a calculus book. The dog's investigative faculties—smelling, tasting, pawing—are simply not the tools that will allow it to make sense of the information held in the calculus book. Likewise, we cannot try to understand things of a higher order by using faculties of a lower order. When confronted with the wisdom of higher mind and intuition, the strategic mind will not be able to make sense of it and will only tear its wisdom apart. The trick of working with the strategic brain is to follow the Wizard's advice: acknowledge its gift for thinking, but remember it doesn't "know" much.

As we prepare to enter the fourth stage of our journey, the approach toward our spiritual nature, we must bring these three lower centers into service to our higher Self. The teaching of the wisdom traditions is that our physical, emotional and mental bodies are the vehicles for bringing our souls into expression in the physical world. These parts of ourselves are not meant to be in charge of the journey or to be pushing us around as we move along the path. The Lion, the Tin Man and the Scarecrow show us that if we get stuck in the shadow side of our lower natures, then fear, emotional drama and mental paralysis will prevent us from moving forward on our soul path.

At the same time, however, we must honor the physical, emotional and mental aspects of ourselves and avoid an ascetic response that cuts us off from these very human parts of our nature. We inhabit physical bodies that need food, water, rest and play. We have exquisite feeling bodies that allow us to engage with life and with other people in the drama and passion of the human experience. We have cognitive abilities that allow us to think, challenge, analyze and construct new ways of seeing and being in the world. These are the gifts of being in human form that we never want to deny or dismiss. These are the capacities that will allow our higher spiritual nature to come into full physical expression in our lives and we need all of these centers activated and alive. As Campbell says, when you get to the fourth story of the building, you don't blow up the lower floors. We must use our human faculties, capacities and experiences as the vehicle for our spiritual work in the world, and we must celebrate our unique human capacity to walk the divinity of our soul into the world of flesh and form.

Stepping Stones

Awareness Affirmation: *I honor the powers and vulnerabilities of my body, emotions and mind. I navigate my path with courage, passion and focus, allowing my expanding spiritual awareness to lead me along the way.*

What events that have recently occurred in your life resonate with this part of the journey?

◎ What fears stop you from taking your place or making yourself at home in your own life story?

◎ How do your unresolved feelings about past experiences or traumas interrupt or dampen your passion about life?

◎ How does your strategic mind create self-doubt or stop you from moving toward your life dream?

◎ Are there parts of yourself—physically, emotionally or intellectually—that you have ignored, cut off from or denied, that are asking for more attention, freedom or expression?

◎ Which of Dorothy's three companions do you most identify with, the Lion, the Tin Man or the Scarecrow and why?

◎ Where are you most likely to get stuck or lost—in your fears, your feelings, or your thoughts?

◎ What have you learned through your life experiences that can help you to move forward when you get stopped?

The Emerald City

"Awe Is What Moves Us Forward."

~ JOSEPH CAMPBELL

Suddenly it seems we are awake and on our way. After the work of the early stages, there is the allure of the clear path opening before us. The helpers have shown us their favor, and we begin to breathe easy. As we move into the fourth stage of our journey, we begin the approach toward our spiritual nature. We have moved through the struggle of confronting our unconscious conditioning and human limitations and enter the expansive space of the heart center. We begin to move out of the energy of "doing" and into the energy of "being." We experience the freedom to be ourselves and to truly embrace the mystery of our being and the majesty of the divine at work in the universe. When we enter our heart, we will find a welcoming and accepting space, for our heart is our center of compassion, forgiveness, inspiration, gratitude and joy. In our heart we can listen deeply to the hardships of the path and find the self-love and self-acceptance we so often seek from others. In our heart we can acknowledge the brokenness of the world and surrender it to the power of the divine. In our heart we can honor the heaviness of life's burdens and lift ourselves up on the wings of grace. In our heart there is time to breathe, to rest, to laugh and to play. In our heart we remember that life is a grand adventure and we can choose to live it with gratitude and joy. As we walk our path,

we can always return to the heart, to this stillpoint, to be renewed,
to be inspired and to remember who we are.

---

*D*orothy emerges from the early stages of her journey with the Emerald City, home of the Great and Powerful Oz, in full view. The city is a glorious, radiant green, and the excitement of nearing what she thinks is the goal of her journey takes hold. She and Toto and her three new companions, the Lion, the Tin Man and the Scarecrow, become so excited that they begin to run toward the Emerald City. Lamenting that none of the other threshold guardians has turned Dorothy back, the Wicked Witch magically creates a field of intoxicating red poppies in the path Dorothy, the Lion, the Tin-Man and the Scarecrow are taking. The Witch makes the vibrant poppies "attractive to the eye," but their enchanted perfume lulls Dorothy, Toto and the Lion into a deep sleep. Unsure and uncertain in the face of this new obstacle, the Tin Man and the Scarecrow cry out for help. In response to their call, Glinda offers assistance in the form of snow to wake the sleeping travelers and allow them to pass through the threshold guardian of the poppies. When they arrive in the Emerald City, they find a happy, joyful, magical place of rest and repose, and a Wizard who is not so great and powerful as they had imagined.

As Dorothy and her friends near the Emerald City, the awe they feel at the sight of the city draws them forward with renewed excitement and enthusiasm. The Emerald City represents the entrance to our spiritual energy, and we are intuitively drawn toward its power. Campbell tells us it is awe that moves us forward on our path, and we feel its power as our Oz friends energetically approach the Emerald City. The early vision of the Emerald City in all its brilliance is a symbol of the early transcendent experiences we all have in life. When we break out of our lower natures and get a glimpse of our higher self and the possibilities that life holds for us, we are pulled by that excitement with great enthusiasm along our soul's path.

Unfortunately, that enthusiasm can be interrupted by threshold guardians. As our friends enthusiastically begin to run toward the Emerald City, the Wicked Witch stops them with a field of enchanted poppies. As the Witch describes, the poppies are "attractive to the eye" but they lull our heroine into a deep sleep. Again we see the work of the threshold guardians that come to stop us on our path to our soul. As we walk the hero's journey and begin to feel the pull of our true spiritual nature, we are often encouraged—by those close to us, by group consciousness, by our fears or insecurities or by the attraction of old patterns, addictions or distractions—to go back to sleep, to go back to our old beliefs and unconscious patterns. Many of us have experiences that heighten our awareness of the spiritual or transcendent parts of our nature and draw us toward a path of spiritual growth. Too often, however, we find ourselves quickly overcome by the "poppy fields" of our life and are lulled back to sleep by the safety and familiarity of our ordinary reality.

We see this pattern of falling asleep at the initial stages of spiritual consciousness in many of the myths. In the

Christ story, as Jesus waits in the Garden of Gethsemani, he asks his disciples to "stay awake" with him as he prepares to walk toward his own experience of transcendence. When Jesus returns from the garden, he finds his followers have all fallen asleep. He says to them, "the spirit is willing but nature is weak" (Matthew 26:41). Like our Oz friends and the disciples of Jesus, our lower natures will be lulled back to sleep as we approach the threshold of our authentic spiritual journey. We are reminded by the symbols of these stories that we must allow our higher Selves to lead us on our path and keep our lower natures awake and aware.

As we approach the Emerald City, the symbol of our higher spiritual Self, we must pay attention to those presences on the path that call us back to sleep. When we feel that pull of confusion or uncertainty, we can cry out for help like our Oz friends and trust that invisible helpers will always appear to assist us in staying awake and moving along our path. Those invisible helpers may come forward in subtle ways, perhaps in the form of encouragement from friends or strangers who seem to recognize the power in the changes we are making and encourage us to keep going. The help may come more dramatically in the opening of doors or opportunities that we believed were not possible. However the help comes, and in whatever form, we learn from the myths that calls for help are always heard and that help will show up in both subtle and dramatic fashion.

Following a sincere call for help on our spiritual journey, we need to remain awake and aware to recognize the openings that appear before us. In the Oz story the Wicked Witch recognizes the presence of the unseen helpers and says, "Curses, somebody always helps that girl." Like Dorothy, we will always have help along the path if we simply stay awake, ask for help and recognize the helpers that appear before us.

Compassion vs. Protection

The Emerald City represents the fourth chakra of the chakra system and the fourth stage of the journey. The fourth chakra is located in the heart and is represented by the color green and the element of air. The fourth chakra is the center of self-love and is the gateway to our higher spiritual energies. The power of the fourth chakra is in our ability to be open-hearted through the energy of compassion and forgiveness for ourselves and others. The spiritual traditions of East and West teach that we can access our higher spiritual nature only through the compassion and self-love of the heart center. Meister Eckhart, the 13th-century Christian mystic whose teachings have bridged East and West, writes that "Compassion clothes the soul with the robe of God and divinely adorns it.... those who follow compassion find life for themselves, justice for their neighbor and glory for God." In the fourth chakra we meet the compassion of God and begin to allow that light to move through us and into the world.

Our weary Oz travelers arrive at the gate of the heart center and are first turned away by the gatekeeper. Their first response to being turned away is disappointment and discouragement. They feel angry and betrayed that they have traveled so far and come through so much and are now being stopped at the gate. This response represents the danger of the fourth chakra. Disappointment, anger, grief, bitterness, resentment and judgment are the human emotions we confront in the lower heart center of the fourth chakra, and these difficult emotions can cause us to close our hearts off in protection, to try to protect our hearts from pain. If we close our hearts in self-protection and get stuck in the negative emotions tied to our seemingly unfulfilled human expectations, we will not gain access to our spiritual inheritance. The spiritual power of the fourth chakra, however, is its ability to receive these difficult emotions of the human experience with compassion, acceptance and love and to transform even our most difficult human struggles by providing the space for healing and transformation.

As our Oz travelers struggle to make sense of this unexpected closed gate on their journey, they remember that Dorothy wears the ruby slippers, the symbol of the soul-directed journey and of the connection to her soul. When they inform the gatekeeper that Dorothy wears the ruby slippers and open themselves to the mystery of the spiritual road they are traveling, they are enthusiastically admitted to the Emerald City. Remember, Glinda cannot wave her magic wand and magically transport Dorothy to the Emerald City. Dorothy has to walk through her old fears, her inner feelings and her conditioned thoughts and beliefs before gaining entry to her heart. As we evolve in our spiritual wisdom, we come to see that challenge and struggle are part of the process of uncovering our deeper self. The teaching of this stage of the journey is that we can enter and inhabit the light of our true spiritual nature only if we have done the work of the three lower centers and come into our hearts connected to our soul. The spiritual task is to remain open hearted, even in times of great trial, trusting that all is well even when we feel confused, abandoned or betrayed by the events of our life. When we grow into this stage of spiritual awareness, we will be received with compassion into our heart center as Dorothy and her friends are received into Oz.

Upon entering the gates of the Emerald City, our Oz travelers first notice the song of joy and laughter ringing throughout the city. The song rings out:

You're out of the woods, you're out of the dark,
you're out of the night.
Step into the light, march into your heart, hold onto
your hope.

People who walk the spiritual path often speak of walking through the "dark night of the soul." For many, the dark night of the soul is the inner work of the first three stages where we face our fears, illusions and inner demons in what feels like a life-and-death struggle. Campbell says that "the dark night of the soul comes just before revelation. When everything is lost, and all seems darkness, then comes the new life and all that is needed." When we look back on our lives at the periods of our greatest struggle and darkness, when it seemed we were completely lost, we often find that these were the periods that propelled us forward into the rich possibilities of our true path. These were the periods that burned away all that was false, illusory and external.

These were the periods that forced us to draw our strength and meaning from the very center of our being. These are often the periods in life when we discover or perhaps remember who we are.

We often emerge from the dark-night period with a lightness and playfulness that is a welcome relief from the earlier struggles. Our Oz visitors have walked through this struggle and enter the Emerald City mesmerized by the wonder and beauty of it all. They are received as honored guests and are encouraged to rest and renew themselves before going forward to meet the Wizard. They are primped and polished until they radiate with freshness and beauty. They are "divinely adorned," as Eckhart says. It is here in the heart center that we have compassion for the struggles of the first stages of the journey and through that compassion discover an internal feeling of lightness and joy that comes with having walked through the darkness and entered the light. This is the beginning of enlightenment. We know we have entered this stage when we begin to see the world with awe, wonder and gratitude, or as Eckhart says, when we begin to "marvel at the beauty of created things and praise the beautiful providence of their Creator."

When we enter this stage we must begin to treat ourselves as honored guests in a sacred world with the care and compassion that is the hallmark of the fourth chakra. When Moses began his walk onto his spiritual path at the foot of the burning bush, he was told, "remove the shoes from your feet, for you are standing on holy ground" (Exodus 3:5). When Jesus was preparing for his transformation into divinity, he had his feet washed by Mary. The symbolic meaning of these stories reminds us that when we enter the fourth chakra, we are confronted by our own divinity. We must acknowledge that where we stand, God stands. We must wash our feet of the limitations of our humanness and the broken stories of our past and know that we indeed stand on holy ground.

The myths and the wisdom traditions clearly teach us that if we are to progress on the spiritual path we must give up our judgment and resistance about the hardships and challenges of our lives. After all, there are no epic myths of conquering heros or compelling resurrection stories without many chapters of struggle and toil. But if we can move with love and acceptance to embrace and integrate all the parts of our life experience, we will find that we can move through all challenges and struggles and that deep transformation and healing are possible when we view our experiences with the spiritual light and compassion of our heart center. When we deeply accept our own divinity, the light of that knowing reveals the light in all beings and the radiance of the world in which we walk. We learn to be gentle with ourselves and gentle with others. We accept that life is a sacred journey of Self-discovery where we are always supported. We experience the breath and inspiration of the divine operating in our life, and we begin to celebrate the whole experience with gratitude and joy. The heart center then becomes a stillpoint, bathed in the light of the divine, where we can rest the parts of our weary human selves, connect with our spirit, restore ourselves for our walk in the world and remember who we are.

Stepping Stones ◉ ◉ ◉ ◦

Awareness Affirmation: *I connect with my own divinity and rest in the care and compassion of my heart center. I gather all my weary parts together in this light to be nourished and restored. I honor the struggles of the journey and celebrate the healing power of my spiritual heart. I am awake with wonder, joy and awe at the beauty of life.*

What events that have recently occurred in your life resonate with this part of the journey?

◉ What are the dark-night experiences you have come through in your life?

◉ What are the seeds of truth that were revealed in those times of struggle?

◉ What are the inner strengths that were uncovered through the struggles?

◉ How are you in need of rest and renewal from these
   struggles?

◉ What are the wonder, joy and awe experiences you have
   had in life?

◉ What are the seeds of truth that were revealed in those
   moments of beauty?

◉ Where in your life do you feel a sense of joyfulness, playfulness and laughter?

◉ Who are the people in your life that seek to pull you back
   into the sleep of the old unconscious patterns?

◎ Who are the people in your life that see and support the emerging parts of your true Self?

◎ When you view the challenging experiences of your life with the love and compassion of the heart center, what spiritual gifts did you receive as you moved through those difficult times?

The Witch's Forest

"What Each Brings Forth Is What Never Before Was on Land or Sea:
The Fulfillment of His Unique Potentialities,
Which Are Different from Anybody Else's."

~ JOSEPH CAMPBELL

When we come into real awareness of our spiritual nature we will
be called to give birth to our higher Self in acts of creative expression in the world. The more practice we have living from the inside
out, the more difficult it becomes to live from the outside in. When
our heart tells us to lead, we will find we can no longer follow.
When our soul knows the immensity of our spirit, we can no longer
make ourselves small. We can no longer pretend that someone else
can do our work, for part of us knows it will not get done if we don't
do it. This is as difficult a time as any on the path. As close as we
are to the truth of our being, the next steps require us to give birth
to parts of ourselves that we have kept hidden from others—and
perhaps hidden from ourselves. The light of our inner being begins
to shine through, and in the face of our own brilliance our first response is to shrink back. It's risky to show that light. It's risky to
show parts of ourselves that we have dared not show. It's risky to
allow the very essence of who we are to come forward into a world
that may not be ready. We look around and hope that someone
bigger, stronger, brighter or braver will show up to do the work that
stands before us. But at this stage in our journey we come to see

that we are all unique expressions of the divine. A part of us knows that we have a gift for the world that no other person can bring into expression: the bigger, stronger, brighter and braver ones can't do what we need to do. A part of us knows that the divine moves into the world through us, and if we refuse to give birth to our higher Self, then God has been stopped from entering the world.

---

*H*aving gained entry to the City of Oz, Dorothy and her friends are again disappointed and despairing as they are denied an audience with the Great and Powerful Wizard of Oz. But following the ominous appearance of the Wicked Witch in the Emerald City writing *Surrender Dorothy* in the sky, Dorothy and her friends are granted their audience with the Wizard in the throne room of the Emerald City. The Wizard declares, "I am Oz, the Great and Powerful, who are you?" Our heroine responds that she is "Dorothy, the small and meek." When our friends make their plaintive requests, they are told that Oz will not help them unless they prove themselves worthy by performing a very small task: Bring him the broom of the Wicked Witch of the West.

When we first approach our spiritual path, we often do so like Dorothy. We metaphorically show up in the throne room of the Great and Powerful Oz and make our requests. We expect that if we present ourselves as *small and meek*, then God will take care of us. From our small self we say our prayers, meditate or perform daily rituals, and then we approach God with our list of needs and desires. We believe that because we said the right prayers, thought the right thoughts or otherwise did what was expected of us, our requests will be magically granted. Some of us place a priest, pastor, guru or spiritual teacher in the role of the wizard. Some of us place a parent, boss or spouse in the role. But most of us begin our spiritual journey in some way hoping and believing that we can avoid the trials and struggles of life through the protection and intercession of an external figure or force with magical powers. The Emerald City is full of this kind of spiritual journeyer, and we see them scurrying throughout the City at any sign of trouble, looking to the Great and Powerful Oz to protect and save them.

But the hero's journey does not leave us in the throne room of an external god in need of magic and protection. The hero's journey calls us into our spiritual maturity. If we truly begin a spiritual journey with earnest intention and attention, we will be pushed forward on our path and into the next and most challenging stage of the journey. We will be called like Dorothy to surrender. We don't have to surrender our power; we have to surrender our attachments to the way we think things ought to be. We will have to surrender our childlike impressions of God. We will have to surrender our need to be magically rescued from our lives. We will have to surrender our small ideas about how our life was supposed to go. We will have to surrender our secret fears about our inadequacies and imperfections. We will have to surrender our fear, anger, regret and disappointment. We will have to surrender our addictions and our resistance. We will have to surrender our need for control or escape. In short, we will have to surrender our most familiar patterns of responding to life, which we have used to keep ourselves safe and protected, because these are the patterns that separate us from our true Self. Surrender means approaching life with a deep-state of acceptance for all that is, knowing that everything we encounter on our path will be used for our highest good if we can release our attachment to our plans.

As we come into our spiritual maturity we will be called to wrestle with the limiting patterns and false beliefs of our *small self* so that we might discover the power and possibilities of our true and divine *Self*. If we have the courage, the passion and the focus for the challenge, we will surrender the small self and discover the seeds of a deep internal spirituality that recognizes the presence and power of God in ourselves and in all things. With this new awareness we no longer need to be protected or rescued from life; instead we recognize that life is our opportunity to stretch, grow, uncover and evolve beyond what our small self saw as possible. We throw off the confinement of the small self and expand more and more fully into the creative potentials of our true Self.

As we make this shift in our perception, the Great and Powerful Oz transforms from the magical wizard into the wise spiritual teacher who sends the seekers back onto the path to walk their unique expression of the divine into the world through an act of creative service. The Wizard, now appearing as sage teacher, gives Dorothy a task. The task, to bring back the broomstick of the Wicked Witch of the West, requires our heroine to go back into the dark forest with her new level of consciousness to face her greatest fear.

She is sent to slay the Witch, as the knights were sent to slay the dragon, as Moses was sent from the fire of the burning bush back to Egypt to confront the power of Pharaoh. As these stories suggest and as Campbell points out, the hero's journey is not for the small, the meek or the faint of heart. The hero's journey is always an adventure fraught with danger where there are no rules, no security and no guarantees. At this stage of the journey we can no longer follow. We must really give birth to our higher Self and learn to live from the very depths of our own interior. We must let go of what is safe and familiar and use our ingenuity and creativity in genuine and authentic acts of service. As Dorothy enters the Witch's forest, which is the gateway for the true spiritual hero, the sign at the entrance reads, "I'd turn back if I were you." And truthfully most of us do.

Creativity vs. Dogmatism

In the terms of the chakra system Dorothy has entered the fifth chakra, the center of authentic and creative expression. The fifth chakra is located in the throat, and its color is light blue. The fifth chakra calls us to drop our external and conditioned identities and to recognize and express our authentic truth in the world from a deep internal sense of identity. Matthew Fox says the birth canal of the higher self resides in the narrow of the throat. In his book *Sins of the Spirit, Blessings of the Flesh* Fox teaches that not giving birth to our higher self through the fifth chakra creates a chasm we desperately try to fill. In the shadow of the fifth chakra we fill this chasm with dogmatism, judgmentalism and addiction to our old patterns. We speak the truth of the small self from its history of trauma and trial, or we speak other people's "truths"—the truths we have been given by family, by friends, by culture, by religion—because that keeps us safe. But if we choose to continue our spiritual evolution through the power of the fifth chakra, we must now use our creative power to give expression to our divine truth. It is in this center that we must surrender our personal will to the Mystery of the Divine Will and begin really saying *yes* to life and to our full and authentic participation in it.

Campbell speaks of this stage as the stage of the spiritual warrior. He tells us that "the warrior's approach is to say 'yes' to life: 'yes' to it all." At this stage we can no longer speak another person's truth; we can only speak and we can only live our own truth. We surrender to the complete mystery of our life unfolding within the complete Mystery of the Divine, and say *yes* to it all; to the joys and the sorrows, to the light and the shadows, to life and to death. The philosopher Heidigger states that "a person is not a thing or a process, but is the opening through which the absolute can manifest." When we surrender in this fifth stage to the Divine Will operating in our lives, we create the opening for the creative expression of the Absolute in the world through us.

As the Oz story continues, Dorothy and her friends accept the Wizard's challenge, steel themselves up for the journey and enter the Witch's Forest to face the Witch. Shortly after entering the forest, they are attacked by the flying monkeys and Dorothy is taken hostage and separated from Toto and her friends in the Witch's tower. The Witch tries to take the slippers from Dorothy's feet but cannot, for she recalls that the slippers will never come off as long as Dorothy is alive. In response to this dilemma, the Witch makes ready for Dorothy's death, which is to come when the hour glass runs out of sand.

Dorothy is captured and held hostage in the castle, metaphorically separated from her helpers by her fear, while time is racing. Here Dorothy faces not only the flying monkeys and the Witch, but the primal human fear, the fear of separation and death in a world of time. The fear of being all alone, vulnerable and running out of time stops many of us from expressing our truth and from living from the core of our being. But remember that the slippers represent Dorothy's soul, and no matter the challenges we face, we are never separated from this inner source of love, creativity, strength and power.

Just as Dorothy is confronted with impending doom, Toto, her intuition, once again reunites her with the internal strengths she earns on her spiritual journey. Toto leads the Lion (Courage), the Tin Man (Passion), and the Scarecrow (Focus) to free her from the tower. Now, freed from her fear and armed with the energies of courage, passion and focus represented by her three mythical companions, she is cornered again by the Wicked Witch. The Wicked Witch in this scene represents the last stand of Dorothy's small self. The small self is the ultimate threshold guardian that resides within each of us. In this epic scene we watch the Wicked Witch goading Dorothy to give in to her deepest feelings of fear and powerlessness as Dorothy, the small and meek. But as the Wicked Witch threatens to destroy her faithful friends, Dorothy forgets her fear and boldly throws the bucket of water. Dorothy forgets her small self and acts instinctively from the power of her true Self. She acts out of love from the center of her being in service to her steadfast friend, the Scarecrow. In the face of sure death, Dorothy makes the internal choice to operate out of love, not fear, and it is that choice which destroys the Wicked Witch and the illusion of separation and death. As the illusion of the Wicked Witch dissolves, Dorothy takes her place as the hero and the once ominous guards transform into friendly presences and escort Dorothy safely back to the Emerald City. Metaphorically, through her act of heroism, she dissolves the illusion of separation and returns to her heart.

When we come into the fifth stage of the journey, we no longer act out of self-interest, self-consciousness or self-protection but from an inner drive to birth our unique gifts into service in the world. At this stage we no longer let anyone—not the naysayers, not our fears, not even the Wicked Witch—stand in our way. Meister Eckhart says that "whatever I want to express in its truest meaning must emerge from within me and pass through an inner form. It cannot come from outside to the inside, but must emerge from within."

Through her travels and trials Dorothy learns that she must begin to trust in and rely on her inner strength and wisdom. As she melts before Dorothy's eyes, the Witch declares, "who would have thought a good little girl like you could destroy my wickedness." When we risk acting from this deep interior place, from the authenticity of the inner

Self in service, the results are always surprising. Dorothy's act of inner truth dissolves the limitations of fear, the illusion of the Witch's invincible power and the illusion of herself as "Dorothy, the small and meek." Much to Dorothy's surprise, she melts the Witch and steps into the truth of the meaning of her name: Dorothy means "Gift from God."

In the challenging trials of this stage of our spiritual evolution we should all be prepared to surprise ourselves. But before we give birth to our deeper selves, we will all feel small and meek. We will all feel outmatched by the challenges in front of us. We will all face the question: Who am I? Who was Dorothy to kill the Witch? Who was Moses to bring the Pharaoh to his knees? Who was David to slay Goliath? Who was Jesus to transform the world? The real question of the fifth stage of our spiritual awakening is, "Who are you *not* to bring the divine into action in the world?" For as Meister Eckhart declares, "Every creature is a word of God."

Otto Rank says, "I must either commit suicide, or I must give birth every day." Rank knew that he either had to give into the deep fear and despair of the small, separate self or give birth through the life-filled creativity of his true Self. If we are to understand and grow into our divinity, we must be willing to surrender our fear of life and our fear of death. If God is to come into being in the world, each of us must recognize that we carry divinity within us and be willing to give birth to our unique expression, our distinctive sound and vibration. Our creative actions birthed into manifestation through our authentic Self are nothing less than pure expressions of the divine. We must remember that if we do not bring the fingerprint of our creative potentials into expression, they will never appear. When our small self cries out in fear to God saying, "Where have you gone?" we are reminded by Eckhart that "God is at home, it is we who have gone out for a walk."

Stepping Stones

Awareness Affirmation: *I give birth each day to more and more of my authentic Self. I move, create, express and act in alignment with my deepest truth and my highest possibilities. I surrender my personal will to the Mystery of the Divine Will and know that all is well.*

What events that have recently occurred in your life resonate with this part of the journey?

◎ What part of you gets stopped in its expression by fear?

◎ What is the fear that stops you from fully expressing who you are?

◎ What challenges lie in the "Witch's Forest" for you to confront?

◎ Where in your history have you risked saying "yes" to life without fear of the consequences?

◎ What are the truths about yourself you have learned on the path so far?

◎ When have you been surprised by your own actions and abilities?

◎ What part of you wants you to say 'yes" to life now?

◎ What do you have to offer to the world as your unique gift of service?

◎ How is the Divine asking you to give birth in your life right now?

Behind the Curtain

"The Goal of the Journey Is to Discover Yourself as Consciousness"

~ JOSEPH CAMPBELL

When we begin to see the world with the wisdom of our soul, the illusions that have held power over us melt away before our eyes. The fears and insecurities that used to stop us in our tracks now appear before us to show us something about ourselves that we need to know. When we are able to see our lives symbolically, through the inner eyes of our soul, we remember that things aren't always as they appear. The Wicked Witch is no longer so ominous, and the Wizard no longer so wise. As the illusions that have controlled our lives and our choices melt away before us, we see spiritual truths buried in the lessons of each day. We begin to understand that everything that occurs in our outer life is a reflection of our inner life. Every experience then becomes an opportunity to expand our consciousness and to incarnate more and more of our own divinity in the world.

In the process of this expansion, we are called to reevaluate the false gods we have created in our lives. False gods give us the illusion of safety, security and protection. We may find them in our jobs, possessions or bank accounts, in our relationships, roles or rituals and in our mentors, teachers, parents and preachers. But as we surrender to our own unfolding, we learn that life is not about safety, security and protection; it is about consciousness, growth and evolution. If we have given away our power to others, we are charged to call it back. If we have built walls around our hearts, we are called to take them down. We are called to face our greatest fears and watch them melt away. We must even look into the eye of God and see how we have made God too small. We must explore all the choices we have made and become aware of how we have created obstacles to the unfolding of our own mystery. We must slay the dragon of ordinary consciousness—which is filled with the illusions of the opposites, separation and death—and expand our consciousness to see clearly with the vision of our inner eye, the truth of who we are.

---

*D*orothy and her friends return to the Emerald City with the broomstick of the Wicked Witch in hand. Dorothy returns to the throne room of the Great and Powerful Oz, stronger and surer of herself, and demands that the Wizard fulfill his promises. As the Wizard bellows and blusters, Toto draws back the curtain to reveal the reality behind the magical façade. Despite the Wizard's admonition to "pay no attention to the man behind the curtain," the illusion of the Great and Powerful Oz is exposed and his illusory power melts away as surely as the illusion of the Wicked Witch. Dorothy now sees the truth of the Wizard, the man behind the curtain. After watching the Wizard dole out fanciful symbols for her friends—a hero's medal for the Lion, a ticking heart for the Tin Man, and an honorary degree for the Scarecrow—Dorothy speaks from her newfound wisdom saying, "there is nothing in that bag for me."

When we pull back the curtain and see with the inner eye of wisdom, we discover the truth of the Buddhist teaching that everything in the outer world is an illusion. We begin to understand that the drama unfolding in our outer life is merely a reflection of our inner struggles. In the darkness of the Witch we find only a symbol of Dorothy's perceived confinement and limitation. In the majesty of the Great and Powerful Oz, we see only a symbol of her feelings of powerlessness and vulnerability. Dorothy's belief in the power of the Witch and the power of the Wizard are both obstacles to her own unfolding. Her willingness to give her power away to things outside of her stops her from knowing the power she possesses within. Yet through her confrontation with the symbols of her inner struggle, she is able to reclaim more and more of herself until she discovers the power at the center of her being. As her own consciousness expands, as she melts the Witch and the Wizard, she also melts her own false identity as "Dorothy, the small and meek."

Consciousness vs. Escapism

This stage of the journey is represented by the sixth chakra. The sixth chakra is located in the center of the forehead, is indigo in color and is represented in symbols by the "third eye"—the eye of the soul. The power of the sixth chakra is consciousness, and its shadow is escapism. The third eye represents the marriage of the right and left brain, the intuition and the intellect, the masculine and feminine ways of knowing and experiencing the world. The sixth chakra allows us to see the whole of things, bringing together our inner world of intuitive knowing with our outer world of logic and reason.

When we move into the sixth chakra, we connect with archetypal images and metaphors. Campbell says that once you understand symbolic sight, you will see symbols everywhere. When we use the power of the sixth chakra to see with symbolic sight, we see the events of our life as opportunities to uncover and expose our self-limiting stories and perceptions. When we see with the intuitive mind, we create new pictures and integrate more and more of what is unfolding before us. In the Oz story, Dorothy's ability to see with symbolic sight melts the illusions of the opposites, of life and death, good and evil, wizard and witch, God and demon. Having seen behind the illusions, Dorothy moves beyond the external symbols to the internal reality they represent. As she incarnates more and more of her own spiritual essence, she embraces the power that resides within.

At this stage in the journey we are called to see all of life with the eye of the soul. The eye of the soul allows us to see beyond the people and the events in our life and to harvest the spiritual truths that are the fruit of our life experiences. When we watch our life with the inner wisdom of the sixth chakra, we see the events of our life as opportunities to come into greater consciousness and to withdraw from the external battles that represent our internal struggles. If we forget that life is a series of spiritual lessons and take the illusions too literally and concretely, the wizards and witches of our fantasies will steal away all the power we were meant to incarnate. We will create images and stories that draw us away from our center and give our power away to others. If we go into the shadow of the sixth chakra, we will use the enormous imaginative power of this center to escape from consciousness and to lose ourselves in the magical thinking, chaos and confusion that is the danger of the intuitive world.

One of the clear lessons of this stage of the journey is not to over identify with the illusion of the symbols in front of us, including our symbols for God. In the Oz story, Toto, Dorothy's intuition, prevents her from making the symbol of the Great and Powerful Oz her god or guru by drawing back the curtain and revealing the limitations of the Wizard. This important revelation allows Dorothy to step beyond the Wizard and continue moving forward on her spiritual path.

A Buddhist teaching says if you meet the Buddha on the street, kill him. Meister Eckhart, a thirteenth century Christian mystic, writes, "I pray God to rid me of God." In the Oz story we find the meaning of these strange parables. The story of the Great and Powerful Oz shows us that we should not make others our gods and that we should not confuse our images of God for God. Our images of God simply point us toward a reality that is always bigger and more mysterious than we can imagine or than another human being can possibly express or hold.

When we come to the sixth chakra we must use our intuition to teach us about God. We have to look at the symbols and the stories that we have adopted to represent God and ask ourselves how we have been conditioned to think about God. Some of us make God too small. We view God as punitive, judgmental, angry or jealous. We decide that, if our life is going badly, then God has either abandoned us or must be punishing us. Some of us make God too big. We keep God in the role of the Great and Powerful Oz and hope that God will show up to rescue us or to bestow great riches and treasures upon us. The problem is that projecting our human stories onto God in this way limits God and our relationship to God. Instead of struggling, exploring and deepening our relationship with God, we put God in a box of our own making. And too often, our stories about God become ways to escape from the work of embracing our highest potential and to forget that we are meant to walk God's power into the world through our personal journey.

Campbell teaches that "God is not an illusion, but a symbol pointing beyond itself to the realization of the mystery of at-one-ment." The eastern traditions allow for the truth that the images we construct to represent the Absolute—God, Allah, Krishna, Buddha, Gaia, Yahweh, Trinity, Christ—are merely a means to point us toward the ultimate and unmanifested reality that is the divine ground of the Universe. But while we use these symbols to move us closer to that ineffable reality, we should not make the mistake of confusing our symbols for the reality, for they will never be big enough to contain the reality of All That Is.

In western religious traditions, we are generally stopped before the symbol of God as The Great and Powerful Oz and in many ways are stopped in our spiritual development by our human interpretations and projections onto that externalized symbol. Too many of us have been taught to metaphorically stand waiting in the throne room for the wizard to reach into his bag of tricks and pull out something for us. Traditional western religious paths do not encourage us to make the leap beyond the symbol to a direct and internal experience of the divine. We must go to the esoteric traditions and to the mystics of the Christian traditions, Meister Eckhart, St. Terese of Avila, St. John of the Cross, Hildegard of Bingen and Julian of Norwich to go past the symbol of God and find the "All in All of Us," the direct experience of the power represented by the symbol. Eckhart says that "God is the spoken and the unspoken, the manifest and the unmanifest." Our symbols can represent only our projections of the manifest reality of God, and our attempts to construct an image of God will always get in the way of letting God be God. As we move into this sixth stage of the journey, we must let go of our images and projections about God, and begin to see that All is God.

We may notice some discomfort when we soften our attachment to our familiar images and stories about God. When our images of God are challenged by life or by the failings of our spiritual leaders, we may feel a bit disenchanted, like Dorothy does as the image of the Great and Powerful Oz dissolves in front of her. But as we allow our constructed images of God to dissolve, we open the space for new and more authentic experiences of God and eventually we allow God to radiate through us. As we let God be God, we come into the experience of God in fuller and fuller appreciation for the power and possibilities in every moment. As we recognize that we are a unit of consciousness, resting within the great consciousness of All That Is, we begin to authentically take our place in the co-creative evolutionary dance that is the purpose of life.

Stepping Stones

Awareness Affirmation: *I experience life through my spiritual senses. I allow the experiences of life to draw me into greater and greater awareness of my relationship with the Divine. I say yes to the co-creative process of Life.*

What events that have recently occurred in your life resonate with this part of the journey?

◎ When you see your life symbolically, how might the events in your outer life be reflecting the struggles or conflicts in your inner life?

◎ How are the outer events in your life trying to raise your consciousness about some aspect of your inner life?

◎ What illusions in your life continue to steal your power?

◎ Where do you allow yourself to give your power away to others?

◎ Describe your familiar images of God?

◎ As you think about God from these images, how does it make you feel?

◎ How do your images of God prevent you from moving forward in your spiritual evolution?

◎ What experiences have you encountered that give you a glimpse of God beyond your images?

The Ruby Slippers

When the illusions melt in front of us, we are confronted with the truth of our own hero nature. Feeling lost, abandoned and forsaken, we come face to face with that which we were seeking when the journey began. We went in search of the magical, the mystical and the divine—and discovered the essence and meaning of life revealed through the struggle and seeking of our human experience. We summoned up the courage to walk into the darkness toward a glimmer of light. We risked the descent into our emotional histories and traumas. We examined the stories and beliefs we had constructed to keep ourselves safe. We offered up our confusion, disillusion, disappointment and grief to the healing compassion of the heart. We nurtured the seeds of our higher creative potentials. We began to see life with the eye of the soul and to participate consciously in the unfolding mystery of the Universe. But did we ever expect to find that we were in fact a ray of the divine light itself? Did we ever expect to see ourselves as the very embodiment of the Absolute in motion? Did we ever expect to discover that we *were one with All That Is, with the original movement of the Universe? When we went looking for God, Allah, Krishna, Gaia, Buddha, Christ, did we ever expect to hear "Thou art That?" Did we ever expect to discover the Om, the sound of the Universe itself, resonating and sounding through our very being?*

---

*I*n the final scenes of the Oz tale Dorothy, disenchanted but not discouraged at the falling away of the illusion of the Great and Powerful Oz, prepares for a more ordinary passage home in the balloon of the magician. Just as they prepare to depart, Toto escapes from the basket of the balloon. Once more Dorothy follows Toto. She leaps out of the balloon and the balloon sets sail without her. In the confusion, the magician floats away unable to take Dorothy on the final stage of her journey. As Dorothy watches him drift out of sight in his balloon, she feels lost, abandoned and despairing as her friends try to console her. But just when all seems lost, the soft pink bubble carrying Glinda appears again out of nowhere. Relieved, Dorothy asks her if she can help her get home. Glinda replies, "You don't need to be helped any longer, you've always had the power to go back to Kansas." The Scarecrow angrily protests, "Why didn't you tell her this before?" To which Glinda replies like a good Zen master, "She wouldn't have believed me. She had to learn it for herself."

In this pivotal scene, Toto leaps from the basket of the balloon just as Dorothy is again surrendering her internal power to the external promise of safety and protection represented by the magician and his ephemeral balloon. Toto leaps from the basket of the balloon as an intuitive message, knowing that in her desire for safety, Dorothy is about to miss the jewel of the hero trip. When all seems lost, in comes Glinda, the heart of compassion, the heart of the soul, providing Dorothy with the guidance she requires. Glinda gently reminds Dorothy that she has always possessed the power she was seeking. The power and potential Dorothy has been seeking from the beginning of her journey does not lie in the hands of Elvira Gulch, Auntie Em, the Wicked Witch, her three faithful friends, the Wizard or even Glinda, her teacher. Dorothy now discovers that her power and potential rests within the very essence of her Being. Glinda embodies the wisdom of this stage of the journey, inviting Dorothy to recognize the seed of God within her—*her Soul.*

With the help of Glinda, Dorothy discovers her connection to the God within—her soul. The symbol of this connection, the ruby slippers, can now take her home. This is the grail of the ancient myths, the discovery of the God within. As Dorothy connects with the power of her own soul, she recognizes her own Buddha or Christ consciousness. The God transcendent is suddenly recognized as the God immanent, the God who lives and breathes and works through each of us as we find our way in the world.

This is the goal of the hero's journey—to discover yourself as consciousness itself—as an emanation of the Divine, connected to All That Is. Campbell calls this discovery the *Apotheosis:*

> *the realization that "I am that which all these other beings are." The hero knows that she is It, the Buddha image, the knower of the truth. "The Kingdom of the Father is spread upon the earth and men do not see it." That's the illumination that comes with Apotheosis.*

While our western religious traditions too often leave us in the throne room of the Great and Powerful Oz, the Oz myth takes us the next crucial steps on our journey where through the use of our own creative and conscious forces we recognize ourselves as connected to the ultimate source of power and love in the universe. Jesus taught this truth, declaring that "The kingdom of heaven is within." Krishna also spoke this truth: "Having pervaded the entire universe with a fragment of himself, he remains." Christian mystic Meister Eckhart echoes the power of this revelation in writing "In this Breakthrough I discover that God and I are one." The Hindu text, the Upanishads, declares that "He is the one God hidden in all beings, all pervading, the Self within all beings." Bede Griffiths, a Catholic monk who lived in India for more than 25 years, bridging eastern and western spirituality, writes, "You look into your self, your body and your mind, and within the depths of your being, beyond your mind, you find this hidden mystery of the Atman, the Spirit.... In Christian terms you have discovered yourself in God. My true Self is my self in God and God in me. I am not really my Self until I have discovered this hidden centre of my being."

Connection vs. Separation

The jewel of the hero's journey is connected to the seventh chakra of the eastern traditions. Through the consciousness of the seventh chakra we become aware of our connection to our Soul and to all that is through the manifest and unmanifest power of God. The seventh chakra is located at the crown of the head and is represented by the color violet. At this stage of the spiritual journey, God is no longer a static being in the sky but the active principle behind all things and within all beings. With this consciousness-altering awareness from our seventh chakra, every act of human creation and expression now becomes an act of God seeding the evolution of consciousness in the world through all. We begin to see all things entwined in a powerful field of unity and connection. The world takes on a numinous quality as we see and experience the light of God within all things.

The shadow of the seventh chakra is the illusion of separation and the denial of the divine unity in which we participate in every moment of our lives. As the magician floats away in his balloon, Dorothy's growing awareness of her Self fades in an instant as the fear of separation and abandonment takes hold. Like Dorothy, when we see ourselves as separate and alone, the world outside appears to be a place of chaos and confusion where we are lost and vulnerable. Like Dorothy, when we get lost in feelings of vulnerability and abandonment, we quickly forget all the lessons of our journey that have pointed us toward a very different reality. But also like Dorothy, we can come to know the God within only through our own experiences and through our own seeking. And when we are finally confronted by the presence of God in all things, in all experiences and in all beings, we also discover the God within.

As Glinda reminds Dorothy of the ruby slippers, the jewel that represents the connection to her soul, Dorothy discovers that she has always had the power to shape her own destiny. The power wasn't outside of her, it was within her. This is the Holy Grail, the presence of God within all things and within all beings, the Om consciousness. Our Soul, symbolized by the ruby slippers, is our ever-present connection to the Om. Griffiths teaches us that "The word *Om* is held to be the original sound. It is a little like the Greek alpha and omega, the beginning and the end which embraces all words, all meaning, all sound, all creation itself." In Christian texts the word *Om* is linked with "the Word" in the Gospel of John: "In the beginning was the Word, and the Word was with God, and the Word was God." Om represents the original vibration, the creative movement of Brahman, of Absolute reality, of the Unmanifest, of God. That first original movement that created all that is and of which we are all a part. When we touch the Om consciousness, we touch the sacred unity that connects all of us to everything. From this field of sacred unity, we know that vulnerability, separation and death are illusions, for nothing ceases to be, all just develops, evolves and expands within the universal field of consciousness. We remember that we are never lost, never separate, never alone. We find our true spiritual home in the *Om!*

Om is the creative, expansive, evolutionary force of the universe. This is the jewel of which Campbell speaks and of which the mystics of all traditions sing. This is the realization Ken Wilbur reveals when he writes "Let a radical realization shine from our faces, and roar from our hearts, and thunder from our brains—this simple fact, this obvious fact: that you, in the very immediateness of your present awareness, are in fact the entire world, in all its frost and fever, in all its glories and grace, in all its triumphs and tears." The truth of the Om consciousness is All in God—the Unity of God immanent and God transcendent—God that pervades all of life and all of our beings and runs through each of us on our every breath, and yet is beyond all, above all and beneath all.

The most important symbol in the Oz story is the ruby slippers. The ruby slippers symbolize the jewel of the hero's journey. They symbolize our ever-present awareness of ourselves as souls in human forms. To connect consciously with our soul is truly the evolutionary key. It is the holy grail. It is our universal "home" in consciousness. We walk the spiral path of consciousness until we make this universal discovery, that at the very center of our being we are bigger than our bodies, bigger than our feelings, bigger than our thoughts and bigger than our life experiences. We discover that we are a soul connected to the source of All That Is.

This discovery allows us to walk through the difficulties, challenges and painful experiences of human life with poise and grace and a deep and eternal knowing that despite all of our disappointments and struggles, all is well. We are participants in a grand mystery designed to move us through our own unfolding, becoming more and more of who we really are. We are connected to our soul and our soul is connected to the source of All That Is—this discovery is the *Om* that sets us free. Once we have touched and rested in this universal home in our consciousness, then all things are possible, every struggle along the path is bearable, every disappointment or darkness can be overcome and we can fully experience the joy and bliss of the path, because truly all is well.

Stepping Stones

Awareness Affirmation: *I am a soul in ever present and eternal connection with All That Is. My soul is a source of love, light and wisdom. I am safe, loved, cared for and protected. I am at home in this center of my being, and all is well.*

What events that have recently occurred in your life resonate with this part of the journey?

◎ As you consider the pivotal moments of your life, how have you been guided toward an awareness of the *Om* within?

◎ When in your life have you experienced a profound sense of connection to the mystical or transcendent?

◎ What feelings, insights and perceptions about yourself grew out of those experiences?

◎ Where in your life do you experience feelings of vulnerability, fear, separation and abandonment?

◎ If you counseled yourself from the wisdom of the seventh chakra, what hidden truth might you discover in those experiences of separation? What might Glinda remind you of?

The Return Home

"The Goal Is To Bring the Jewel Back to the World,
To Join the Two Things Back Together."

~ Joseph Campbell

The Holy Grail symbolizes the quest for the highest spiritual fulfillment of a human life. Along the path we learn that each life represents a unique form of expression of the Divine Reality itself. We
also learn that it is the hero's calling not only to find the bliss but to
bring the bliss back and to live it in the world. But to live this truth
in the world is no easier a task than it was to discover it. When we
have touched the highest parts of ourselves, the God within and
without, it is often hard to live in the gap between this world and
that world. We come back into this world light and alive. We see
the magic of that light in every being. We understand the struggles
of others, for we have walked those struggles ourselves. We see the
mystery of the Divine Field of Being unfolding moment to moment
in All That Is. But this view is not what most of the world sees. The
world is not prepared to honor this way of seeing and knowing.
And yet somehow we are meant to walk this truth into the world.
We can't stay in the woods, in the desert or on the mountain top. If
God is going to walk into the world and change it, that change must
come through us—through our willingness to live in the Mystery
and to give witness to the Mystery. Where we walk, God walks.
Where we create, God creates. Where we evolve, our ability to

make God manifest in us and in the world evolves. Ready or not, we must walk with our jewel back into the world.

---

*A*s Dorothy prepares to leave the Land of Oz, Glinda asks her what she has learned on her travels. Dorothy responds by saying, "If I'm going to go looking for my heart's desire, I won't look any farther than my own backyard, because if it's not there, I've never lost it to begin with." With that knowledge Dorothy is ready to return home on her own power. As Dorothy prepares for the journey home, Glinda swirls her magic wand over the top of Dorothy's head and tells her to click her heels together three times repeating "there's no place like home." Dorothy awakens back in Kansas, at the point where her hero's journey began, surrounded by her family and friends.

As Campbell promised, myths provide us with the symbols that allow us to make the connection between our waking consciousness and the sheer mystery of the universe. If the hero's journey requires us to walk back into the world with our jewel, it is fitting that in the symbolism of the Oz adventure Dorothy wears the symbol of the jewel on her feet. Glinda waves the wand over Dorothy's head while Dorothy clicks her heels together three times. The three clicks represent the triune nature of the human experience—personality, Soul and Spirit aligned in mystical unity and connection. The pairing of the wand over her head and the clicking of her heels symbolically connects the seventh chakra with the first chakra in that endless cycle of transcendence and return. For once we have an authentic transformative experience, we must walk our new consciousness back into the world and live it. Wilbur tells us that "authenticity always and absolutely carries a *demand* and a *duty*: You must speak out, to the best of your ability, and shake the spiritual tree, and shine your headlights into the eyes of the complacent. You must let that radical realization rumble through your veins and rattle those around you." For "only by investing and speaking your vision with passion can the truth one way or another finally penetrate the reluctance of the world."

In the last stage of the hero's journey, like Dorothy we gather up the lessons of the path and are returned to the place where we began our journey—changed, grateful, awake and alive. At this stage of the journey we embrace a new Godview—knowing the God within, not just the God without—God immanent, not just God transcendent. We embody the knowledge of a God who lives and moves through our willingness to walk back into the world and change it by our very presence, giving witness to the Presence. That's the Om: the God in all things; the God so vast and so unimaginable and yet so personally present within all things; the God so magnificent and powerful and yet so dependent on our waking up to our own Christ or Buddha consciousness; the God that is the ground of all consciousness that depends on human participation in the evolution of consciousness; the profound awareness that I Am That.

We see the world now with new eyes, with the eyes of the mystic, alive and sparkling with the special awareness of the Infinite in motion through the wonder of the universe.

But we must return to the place where we began to complete the hero's journey. We must re-enter the world where we began and live our new truth. In the eastern tradition this is the return from the seventh chakra to the first. Poet T.S. Elliot writes, "My end is my beginning." In the Old Testament story it is Moses returning transformed from the mountaintop. In the Oz myth, Dorothy realizes that the path of her life is always right before her, not *somewhere over the rainbow*, and she returns to Kansas. The teaching of the myths and of the religious traditions is clear; we do not get to stay at the top of the mountain. Eckhart says that "God waits on human history, and suffers as she waits." God depends on us to re-enter the world and transform it by our presence. This is the evolutionary demand of God immanent.

Campbell warns us, however, that "the great problem is bringing life back into the wasteland where people live inauthentically. Bringing back the gift to integrate it into a rational life is very difficult." We see even in the first moments of Dorothy's return the confusion and lack of understanding from those around her when she tries to explain her experiences and to share her new truth in her old world. Auntie Em, Uncle Henry, the farmhands and the local magician chuckle politely and humor Dorothy as she tries to speak about the depth of her transformation. Like Dorothy, when we try to explain to others what we have come to know through our deep experiences of the divine, they will not understand it until they learn it for themselves. On the cross Jesus cries out, "Father, forgive them, they know not what they do." These stories remind us that the world is not always ready to accept deep spiritual truth. So when we return with the jewel, Campbell tells us we have three apparent choices:

> *The first choice is the refusal of the return. We realize that "people look at us with glassy eyes, and call us a 'kook' and so we retreat." We buy a place in the woods and try to hold onto the bliss state in isolation and seclusion.*
>
> *The second choice is to give people what they want—to convert the truth into a form that will be accepted and comfortable, and to sell it in some commercial way. Again he tells us we have renounced the jewel.*
>
> *The third possibility, the only real honoring of the jewel, is to find some portion or aspect of the domain into which you have come which can accept some portion of the truth you have to present. It requires a good deal of compassion and patience. Look for the cracks in the wall and give only to those who are ready to receive."*

Campbell teaches that while it surely takes courage to return after you've been in those woods or on that mountaintop, you really do not have a full adventure unless you come back into the world. Ultimately this is the task. Campbell reminds us, "the bodhisattva, the one whose being is enlightened, voluntarily comes back into the world, knowing that it's a mess, and participates joyfully in the sorrows of the world." Eckhart tells us, "God does not ask anything else of you except that you let yourself go and let God be God in you."

Finally, the myths and traditions teach us that the hero's journey is not a single adventure: it is a series of adventures. The philosopher Heraclitus says that "you cannot discover the limits of soul, even if you travel every road to do so; such is the depth of its meaning." For just when we think we know the truth, we are called into the next level of opening in the Mystery of the Field of Being within which we live and breathe and make our meaning. The power of the myth of the hero's journey is the "waking of individuals in the knowledge of themselves, not simply as egos fighting for a place on the surface of this beautiful planet, but equally as centers of Mind at Large—each in his own way at one with all." We will take the hero's journey again and again, always evolving and expanding into the sea of divine consciousness, and then walking our piece of the Om consciousness back into the world to share with those who are ready to receive it.

Stepping Stones

Awareness Affirmation: *I am always at home in the Om. I am one with the divine light and love of God. I walk my path in deep awareness of that eternal connection. I am a source of light and love in action*

What events that have recently occurred in your life resonate with this part of the journey?

◉ In what ways are you being called to walk your truth back into the world?

◉ What stops you from returning to the world and speaking your truth?

◉ In what ways are you bringing the Om consciousness into expression in your daily life?

◎ What truths can you now speak without blame or resentment?

◎ What practices can you maintain in your daily life that will help you to remember who you are and your connection to God?

The Practice

"Life Is a Mystery to Be Lived, Not a Problem to Be Solved"

~ WILLIAM BUTLER YEATS

I was raised by an amazing mother who was also named Dorothy, and her favorite admonition to her children when we faced times of struggle, hardship or confusion was this: "Life is a mystery to be lived." My mother learned this truth from walking her own yellow brick road, and it is a truth that all of us who journey to find our home will discover. We are always at home in a great Mystery that is unfolding through us and around us. The lesson of Dorothy's hero's journey is that we no longer need to search for our life or for our power in remote and distant places. We need to remember that our life unfolds mysteriously in front of us following the call of our soul from our home in the center of our being. Our work is to follow our intuition, to stay present to the mystery unfolding before us and to trust God enough to take our place in the world each day with an open heart. The powerful lessons of the Oz myth, the hero's journey, and the wisdom of the chakras give us guidance to make our way along the spiral path that opens before each of us. The spiral path moves us out into the world of experiences, the Oz, and then spirals in toward our true Self, our home in the Om. Here are the lessons for everyday living that we can draw upon as we put on our ruby slippers and prepare to make our own epic journey

I. Find the **COURAGE** to stand in your own life story and to walk your hero's journey.

Courage and resolve are foundational to the hero's journey. Dorothy's story reminds us that the spiritual journey home is not for the faint of heart or the small and meek. Sri Aurobindo, eastern teacher and mystic, counsels those on the spiritual journey that "to remain quiet within, firm in the will to go through, refusing to be disturbed or discouraged by difficulties or fluctuations, that is one of the first things to be learned on the Path." If we panic and run at any sign of difficulty or distress or see disaster and darkness lurking behind every corner, we won't even begin to walk our path. Aurobindo counsels a quiet and steady courage that will move us steadily along our way.

The Cowardly Lion cannot take his place as king of the forest and we cannot take our place at the center of our story without spiritual courage. As the Wizard advises the Lion, living with courage does not mean we will be free from fear at this early stage of the process. It means that there is something solid and true at the core of our being that reminds us to push on and to push through our fear. We learn from the Oz adventure that the things we are most afraid of are generally illusions of our own conditioning and limitations of our own minds. When we summon our courage to push

through the fear, the illusions and limitations dissolve
before us and we move forward on our journey.

2. Harness the **PASSION** of your feelings and vital life energy in the present moment.

Our feelings are a gift. In the present moment our feelings gently steer us away from the negative and un-
pleasant and toward the uplifting and satisfying. Our
feelings soar in the happy and momentous experiences
of life, and they fall during times of suffering and loss.
Our feelings give us the goose-bumps and excitement
when something seems right and the pit in our stomach
or tension in our chest when something is awry. Our
feelings help us to pay close attention to each step of our
journey and to make sense of our experiences along our
path. Our feelings and passion for life help us connect
to the deeper and richer parts of our journey and to the
people who walk most closely with us along our way.

The danger is that our feelings and thoughts can get
tangled up together to create powerful and toxic emotions. Emotions are connected to the experiences of our
past. Emotions have the power to flood our senses, and
we can drown in these deep waters and lose our way.
If we are repeatedly reliving the painful experiences of
our past through the toxic and paralyzing emotions
we have created, we will be frozen in time along our
spiritual journey like the Tin Man who is found frozen
along the journey to Oz. My friend and teacher in the
energy of emotions, Carol Ritberger, writes that "if you

hold on to old emotional hurts, fears and life's traumas, then you use up enormous amounts of energy trying to sustain something that in reality is really disconnecting you from your life.... Holding onto any emotion that does not serve you well makes no sense at all because it will rob you of everything: quality of life, energy, good health, enjoyment, love, happiness, joy, peace, meaningful relationships and abundance—All the things that both God and our spiritual selves believe we are worthy of having in this lifetime."

We can learn from the Oz adventure that we must be wary of getting disconnected and paralyzed in the purgatory of toxic emotions and traumas from our past. The old French root of the word *purgatory* means "place of cleansing." If we can remember that every experience of life is an opportunity to remember who we are and to connect more deeply with our truest Self, we can learn the lessons of our past, cleanse the toxic emotions that are keeping us stuck and fully engage in the journey before us. Our passion and energy for life and our present moment feeling senses will be marvelous sources of wisdom and guidance as we make our way to our spiritual home.

3. Use your strategic mind to **FOCUS** on your life dream and to cut through illusions and limiting beliefs.

Our strategic minds are phenomenal at making plans, asking questions, conducting research, analyzing problems and collecting knowledge. Our minds can help us to concentrate, focus and prioritize in a world of dizzying distractions. The trick of working with the strategic brain, however, is to follow the Wizard's advice and remember it doesn't "know" much. If we are going to set out on the spiritual journey, into the eye of the great Mystery of life, we need to know that it will not make sense, it will not be logical and it is beyond our ability to understand. The cosmic questions cannot be answered, they can only be lived and experienced. On the journey home we will meet the transcendent, the numinous and the ephemeral, and our strategic brain will be of no use in that atmosphere.

While I know that my mind can be a source of great focus and concentration, I also know that it can create a firestorm of doubt and confusion. Our minds are all capable of disabling and destructive thinking patterns. Neuropsychologist Joan Borysenko vividly described the destructive power of the mind in a book for our times, *Fried,* saying that "a neurotic thinking pattern is negative, self-critical, hopeless, helpless and blaming." As we walk along the spiritual path, the neurotic habits of our mind will derail us as powerfully as our toxic emotions. But our minds are also capable of recognizing patterns, even our own self-destructive patterns, and we can catch ourselves in the act and choose new thoughts and more empowering strategies.

Our strategic minds are also excellent at studying and learning. If we can get clear about some of the operating principles along the spiritual journey, then we can be more prepared for what lies ahead and more conscious as we travel. I have spent the last thirty years or more reading and studying the psychological, philosophical and spiritual texts and teachers of all traditions, and you see the trails of those teachers weaving throughout this book. My personality is hard wired for logic and analysis and I have been helped immensely by the writings and teachings of those who have walked this Mystery before me. They remind me to suspend my critical mind and to engage my mystic mind, to trust my deepest intuitions even in the absence of objective proof, to open to a wider and deeper source of wisdom and truth and to live in constant relationship with the unknown and the unseen.

The wisdom of the Oz adventure is to let your mind help you focus and concentrate on the path in front of you, but don't let it create a firestorm of self-doubt and distraction. Let yourself study and learn from wise masters and mystics of the path, and don't disable yourself with questions and contradictions. Most importantly, remember what the Wizard says to the Scarecrow when he asks for brains, "You don't need them. You learn something every day. Experience is the only thing that brings knowledge, and the longer you are on earth, the more experience you are sure to get." Relax your mind enough to enjoy the journey and trust that the deeper wisdom we seek will be gained through our experiences along the way.

4. Renew yourself in the **COMPASSION** center of your heart so you can follow this path with love, light, inspiration, gratitude and joy.

The fourth stage of the journey is marked in the Oz adventure by the entry into the Emerald City. The Emerald City sparkles with light, magic and beauty. It rings with bells, music and singing. It is the place where the travelers find welcome, rest and renewal. The Emerald City is the symbol of the heart center. The fundamental energy of the heart center is love. The spiritual teachers of all times teach us that we really only have two choices on our spiritual journey: Love or Fear. Elizabeth Kubler Ross and David Kessler talk about love like this: "Love, that thing we have great difficulty even describing, is the only truly real and lasting experience of life. It is the opposite of fear, the essence of relationships, the core of creativity, the grace of power, an intricate part of who we are. It is the source of happiness, the energy that connects us and that lives within us."

Our heart centers are the real opening to our spiritual selves. Until we enter the energy of our heart we really are just weary travelers along the difficult path of life. But when we enter our hearts, something opens up inside of us and we find a source of life and renewal that can prepare us for the deeper turns along the path and sustain us as we make our way across the travails. The heart is the center of compassion, gratitude, inspiration, forgiveness and joy. It is a place of connection and healing where we can gather together all of our weary and confused parts and find a place to breathe ourselves back into wholeness. It is truly the place where we *re-member* who we are.

The danger of this center is that we may not want to leave it. After what may seem to have been a long and arduous journey, we are so grateful to be received into this safe and loving space that we are not anxious to make ourselves vulnerable again by venturing on our way. In the Oz adventure we see Dorothy and her friends, along with the citizens of Oz, using the walls of the Emerald City as a place of protection and a fortress against the outside world. But the Wizard sends Dorothy along her way, needing only the protection of her soul, the ruby slippers, to continue safely along her journey.

Like Dorothy, after opening the door to our spiritual selves we are all called to continue on our way. But our entry into the heart center creates a new stillpoint to which we will return again and again. Our prayer, centering or meditation practices help us to regularly reconnect with the energy of our heart. We receive ourselves in the heart with great compassion for the trials and challenges we experience on our journey. We find the pearls of wisdom and light we uncovered along the way and we have gratitude for the gifts of all of our experiences. We breathe deeply into all of our parts, inspiring our bodies, emotions, minds and spirits. We forgive ourselves and others for the difficulties and disturbances along the way, and we experience the joy and lightness of a heart that is grand enough to hold it all in a loving embrace. As we walk from this point forward, we must remember to anchor ourselves in this energy of the heart and to regularly return here for balance, rest and renewal.

5. Express your **CREATIVITY** and power from your own center, giving birth to your truth.

Creativity is at the core of the spiritual journey. The wisdom traditions teach that each of us is a unique expression of the divine and it is our calling to find and discover our truth. Sri Aurobindo taught that "the object of the divine life is to realize one's highest self or to realize God, and to put the whole being into harmony with the truth of the highest self or the law of the divine nature, to find one's own divine capacities great or small and fulfill them in life as a sacrifice to the highest or as a true instrument of the divine."

As we learn from the Oz adventure, we don't get to stay inside the protection of the Emerald City as one of the crowd. We will be asked to step forward, each in our own way, to give expression to our highest possibilities. When we are called to create from the center of our being we will be challenged like Dorothy to face our deepest fear: that we are small and meek and not up to the task. When they begin, all of the Oz characters work on a deficit model: the Lion lacks courage, the Tin Man lacks heart, the Scarecrow lacks brains and Dorothy has lost her home; the Witch needs the ruby slippers to have power, and the Wizard needs the illusions to be wise. Our small selves operate in deficits, scarcities, and *not enough* stories that will stop us in our tracks. Our small selves use narrow-mindedness, dogmatism and judgment to enforce the limiting beliefs that stand in our way.

The Oz adventure reminds us that we must surrender our small selves, our small ideas, our small judgments and our small stories for our lives. We must be willing to take our authentic place in our story, to live from that burgeoning truth at the center of our being, and to bring our divine gifts, talents and powers into the world. Deepak Chopra teaches that "to be really free, there is no option but to be yourself. You are the living center around which every event happens. By being yourself you open the door to *what is*, the never ending play of cosmic intelligence curving back to know itself again and again." All of our Oz characters had to discover that what they thought they lacked was always inside of them. If we wish to travel the spiritual path, we will have to be prepared to slay the illusions of powerlessness and limitation that stand prepared to defeat us, and to surrender to the unfolding of our soul through every step of our journey.

6. Expand your **CONSCIOUSNESS** by seeing the journey with symbolic sight.

At this stage of the journey we engage our wisdom mind and our mystic's eye as we travel more securely along the spiritual path. We start to see our journey with symbolic sight. Symbolic sight is a tool of our spiritual senses. We let go of our attachments to our pleasures or our pains and we look for the truth behind the curtain of illusion and for the symbols and metaphors that illuminate our everyday experiences. We ask what new truth is emerging and what lies hidden or unseen behind the patterns of our lives. We trust that our journey is guided and that behind every experience is a divine spark of light and an opportunity to grow and unfold in our spiritual consciousness.

The danger of this stage is that we retreat into the magician's world of magic without taking responsibility to hold our own as we walk along the path. Glinda reminds us that there were no magic tricks that could have moved Dorothy more quickly along her journey home. She needed to walk it on her own power and with her ever-expanding awareness if she was going to find her way home. Chopra reminds us that at a certain stage "almost anyone who strives spiritually must become his or her own guide." There is a spiritual maturity that is required to navigate this path. We may begin walking our path as spiritual children waiting for magicians, good witches and wizards to transport us to the destination, but if we do our work along the way, we emerge as wise sages able to traverse the uncertainties and paradoxes of the path with poise and wisdom from our own center. Let your wisdom mind and your mystic's eye give you clarity about the patterns and symbolic messages of your life and guide you along your way.

7. Remember your **CONNECTION** to all that is.

At this stage of the journey we experience a sacred unity with *All That Is*. We recognize that the possibilities of the universe flow through us and we will always receive help if we ask. We resist the story that we are all alone, because we know that we are all one, eternally connected in the sacred Mystery of Life. In this awareness fear dissolves, love permeates and we join effortlessly in the cosmic dance. With this sense of purpose and poise we can embody this powerful affirmation by spiritual teacher Louise Hay:

In the infinity of life where I am,
all is perfect, whole and complete.
I believe in a power far greater than I am
that flows through me every moment of the day.
I open myself to the wisdom within,
knowing that there is only One Intelligence in this Universe.
Out of this One Intelligence comes all the answers,
all the solutions, all the healings, all the new creations.
I trust this Power and Intelligence
knowing that whatever I need to know is revealed to me,
and that whatever I need comes to me
in the right time, space and sequence.
All is well in my world.

8. **WALK** your divinity into the world.

Having made your way Home, you recognize that you are a manifestation of God and that love, joy and connection are your birthright. You come to know yourself as an expression of the OM consciousness, knowing from your core that *I Am That*, and you stand prepared to walk the journey of that unfolding divinity into the world as a transformative process and presence. The myths and legends teach us that we do not get to stay on the mountaintop. The great mindfulness master, Thich Nhat Hanh, writes that "Every morning, when we wake up, we have twenty-four brand new hours to live. What a precious gift! We have the capacity to live in a way that these twenty-four hours will bring peace, joy, and happiness to ourselves and others." This is our work as bodhisattvas, as those who are enlightened, to return to the space of our ordinary lives, to the place where our journey began, and to share our light with others.

The trip from Oz to Om is from the outside to the inside; from a focus on finding our happiness, peace and joy in things outside of ourselves, to finding those treasures lying within as the essence and ground of our being. Moving through these evolutionary stages does not occur of its own accord. We must participate in our own unfolding. Bear in mind that evolution is a process, and progress on the path requires a clear intention, a contemplative practice, a healthy dose of self-awareness and the patience and perseverance to walk the path. Dare to be the hero of your own life story, while remembering that the hero's journey will take you on a path that is not for cowards, for the small and meek, for the faint of heart or for those without the focus and fire of the soul. We must walk the path moment by moment and day by day with as much consciousness as we can muster. We will confront obstacles. We will be challenged. There will be struggles. But remember that the obstacles, challenges and struggles are invitations to go deeper and to make choices that are more aligned with our soul's intentions. If we hold onto the markers of the hero's journey, we can make those choices with more awareness and faith, trusting that if we surrender to the unfolding process of life we will move into greater and greater consciousness as we go.

In the end, Dorothy is transported home by the sheer power of saying "there's no place like home." There is no power on earth like the power of taking your place in your own story, from your "h*OM*e" in the center of your Being. All things are possible from that place. Miracles happen from that place. Doors fly open from that place. You are the hero of your own story. Walk your life like the hero of the greatest myth and the most amazing mystery ever told. The privilege of a lifetime truly is being who you are. Wake up! Follow your bliss! The universe depends upon it!

Lessons from Oz

1. Things are not as they appear—look beyond and below the surface of things to find the deeper meaning.

2. Your fears are just illusions built on false perceptions—*lions and tigers and bears oh my!*—don't let them run away with you.

3. Keep your feelings moving to guide you in new directions—don't let your emotions paralyze you or keep you stuck.

4. Remember, your small "brain" doesn't know much—don't let it manage things.

5. Negative thoughts and limiting beliefs are like flying monkeys—don't take them too seriously—face them with your soul and they will transform in the face of true power.

6. The ego—small self—is like the wicked witch—she loses power and eventually melts away as you awaken to your soul and re-member who you are.

7. Listen to your intuition—it is your soul's voice and your guide to spiritual growth and evolution—don't go to sleep in the poppies.

8. Call for help when you need it—you are never alone—you are always held in the loving embrace of the divine—gently and lovingly led to where you need to be.

9. You must open your heart to be admitted to your soul's kingdom—your heart connected to your soul is all you need for the journey.

10. Regular time in the energy of your soul refreshes and restores you—spend time here each day in prayer or meditation preparing for the more potent parts of your journey.

Remember—we are all kings and queens of light and love.
Bring all of your parts with you in service to your soul's purpose
Find your home in the OM!

For a full color copy of this page, please visit www.tracybowe.com

The Seven Chakras

	Chakra Centers	Chakra Powers	Chakra Shadows
7	Guidance	Connection	Separation
6	Intuition	Consciousness	Escapism
5	Expression	Creativity	Dogmatism
4	Heart	Compassion	Protection
3	Mental	Focus	Firestorm
2	Emotional	Passion	Purgatory
1	Physical	Courage	Fear

For a full color copy of this page, please visit www.tracybowe.com

Bibliography

Baum, L. Frank. *The Wizard of Oz*. London: Octopus Books Limited, 1985.

Borysenko, Joan. *Fried*. Carlsbad: Hay House, 2011.

Chopra, Deepak. *How to Know God. The Soul's Journey into the Mystery of Mysteries*. New York: Harmony Books, 2000.

Fox, Matthew. *Passion for Creation: The Earth Honoring Spirituality of Meister Eckhart*. Rochester: Inner Traditions International, 2000.

Fox, Matthew. *Meditations with Meister Eckhart*. Rochester: Bear and Company, 1983.

Fox, Matthew. *One River, Many Wells*. New York: Jeremy P. Tarcher/ Putnam, 2000.

Fox, Matthew. *Sins of the Spirit, Blessings of the Flesh: Lessons for Transforming Evil in the Soul and Society*. New York: Three Rivers Press, 2000.

Kubler-Ross, Elisabeth and Kessler, David. *Life Lessons: Two Experts on Death and Dying Teach Us About the Mysteries of Life and Living*. New York: Scribner, 2000.

Griffiths, Bede. *The Cosmic Revelation: The Hindu Way to God*. Springfield: Templegate Publishers, 1983.

Hay, Louise. *You Can Heal Your Life*. Carlsbad: Hay House, 1999.

Myss, Caroline. *Anatomy of the Spirit: The Seven Stages of Power and Healing*. New York: Three Rivers Press, 1996.

O'Donohue, John. *Eternal Echoes: Celtic Reflections on our Yearning to Belong*. New York: Cliff Street Books, 1999

Osbon, Diane K. *Reflections on the Art of Living: A Joseph Campbell Companion*. New York: HarperCollins Publishers, 1991.

Palmer, Parker. *Let Your Life Speak: Listening for the Voice of Vocation*. San Francisco: Jossey-Bass, 1991

Ritberger, Carol. *Your Personality, Your Health*. Carlsbad: Hay House, 1998.

Sri Aurobindo. *Growing Within: The Psychology of Inner Development.* Twin Lakes: Lotus Press, 1992.

Sri Aurobindo. *The Integral Yoga: Sri Aurobindo's teachings and method of practice.* Twin Lakes: Lotus Press, 1993.

Hanh, Thich Naht. *Peace is Every Step: The path of Mindfulness in Daily Life.* New York: Bantam Books, 1991.

Whyte, David. *The Heart Aroused: Poetry and the Preservation of the Soul in Corporate America.* New York: Currency Doubleday, 1994.

Wilbur, Ken. *One Taste: The Journals of Ken Wilbur.* Boston: Shambhala, 1999.

Wilbur, Ken. *The Simple Feeling of Being: Embracing Your True Nature.* Boston: Shambhala, 2004.

About the Author

Tracy Flynn Bowe, J.D., M.A., has
a Bachelor's Degree in Psychology
and Theology from the College of
St. Benedict, a law degree from
the University of Minnesota, and
a Master's Degree in Counseling
Psychology from the University
of St. Thomas. She is a co-creator
and teacher of the SEND Program
with her sisters, and the author of
The Land Beyond Forever and *Cre-*
ate the Life You Imagine: What are You Waiting For. With
her husband of 30 years, she is the parent of four children
and lives on the Mississippi River in Central Minnesota.

With professional experience as a lawyer, mediator, con-
sultant, educational leader, counselor, and coach, she brings
her life experience and talent to her work as a speaker,
teacher and author on topics of holistic health, integrated
psychology and spirituality. Tracy encourages clients, readers and audiences to live with consciousness and empow-
erment and to create life and vocational paths that support
their unique talents, their highest aspirations and the unfolding of love and consciousness in the world.

For more information about her work visit www.tracy
bowe.com.

61775451R00088

Made in the USA
Lexington, KY
20 March 2017